CHIVALRY

CHIVALRY

Story and Words
NEIL GAIMAN

*Adaptation, Art, and
Illuminated Manuscript Lettering*
COLLEEN DORAN

Lettering
TODD KLEIN

DARK HORSE BOOKS

MIKE RICHARDSON
President and Publisher

DANIEL CHABON
Editor

CHUCK HOWITT and KONNER KNUDSEN
Assistant Editors

PATRICK SATTERFIELD
Designer

ADAM PRUETT and BETSY HOWITT
Digital Art Technicians

Published by Dark Horse Books
A division of Dark Horse Comics LLC
10956 SE Main Street ❖ Milwaukie, OR 97222

DarkHorse.com

To find a comic shop in your area, check out the Comic Shop Locator Service: comicshoplocator.com

First edition: March 2022
Ebook ISBN 978-1-50671-912-2
Hardcover ISBN 978-1-50671-911-5

1 3 5 7 9 10 8 6 4 2
Printed in China

Library of Congress Cataloging-in-Publication Data

Names: Gaiman, Neil, author. | Doran, Colleen, 1963- artist. | Klein, Todd, letterer.
Title: Chivalry / Neil Gaiman, story and words ; Colleen Doran ; adaptation and art ; Todd Klein, lettering.
Description: First edition. | Milwaukie, OR : Dark Horse Books, 2021. | Audience: Ages 12+ | Audience: Grades 7-9 | Summary: "An elderly British widow buys what turns out to be the Holy Grail from a second-hand shop setting her off on an epic visit from an ancient knight who lures her with ancient relics in hope for winning the cup"-- Provided by publisher.
Identifiers: LCCN 2021010115 (print) | LCCN 2021010116 (ebook) | ISBN 9781506719115 (hardcover) | ISBN 9781506719122 (ebook)
Subjects: LCSH: Graphic novels. | CYAC: Graphic novels. | Fantasy. | Knights and knighthood--Fiction.
Classification: LCC PZ7.7.G27 C47 2021 (print) | LCC PZ7.7.G27 (ebook) | DDC 741.5/942--dc23
LC record available at https://lccn.loc.gov/2021010115
LC ebook record available at https://lccn.loc.gov/2021010116

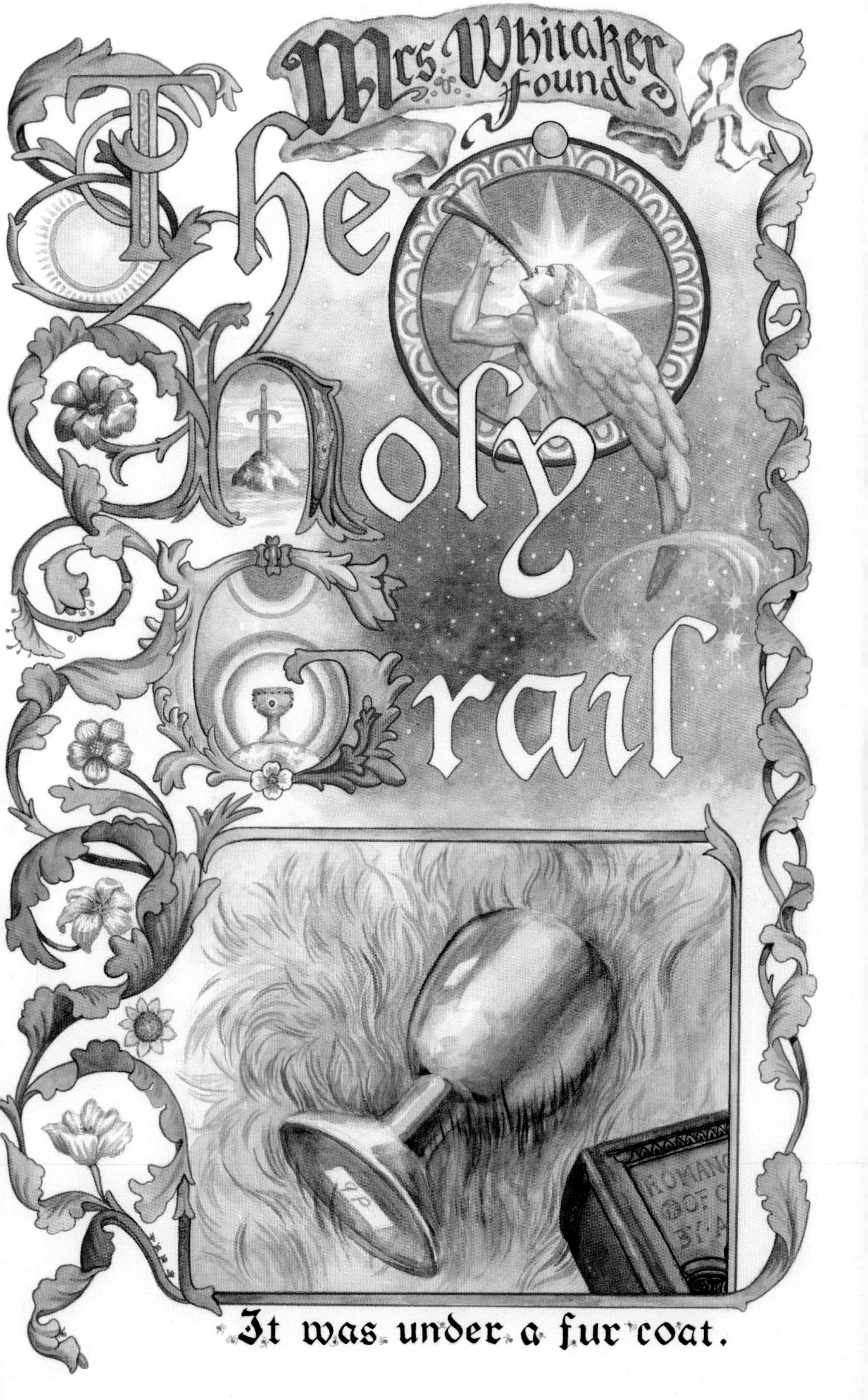
Mrs Whitaker Found
The Holy Grail

It was under a fur coat.

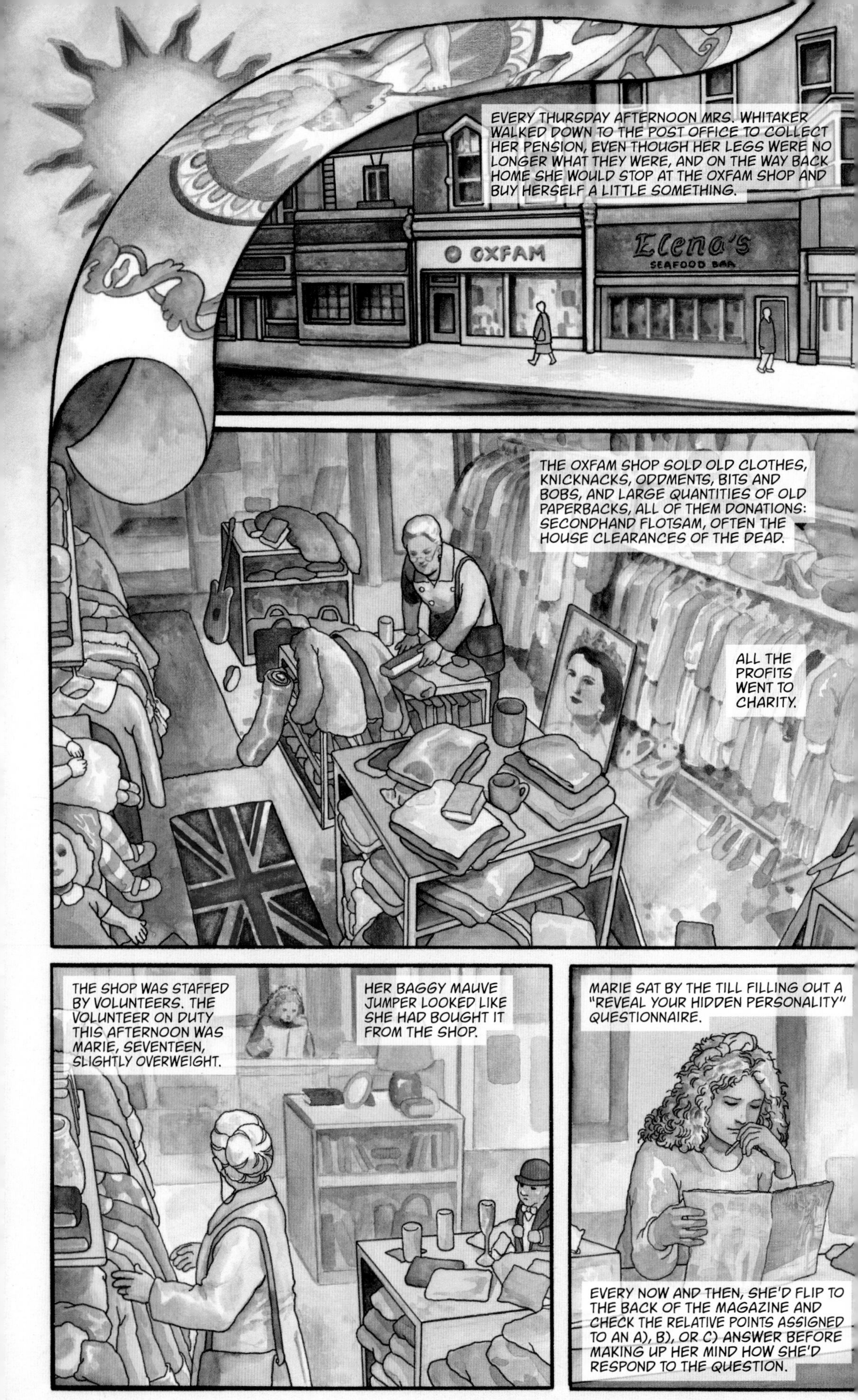

EVERY THURSDAY AFTERNOON MRS. WHITAKER WALKED DOWN TO THE POST OFFICE TO COLLECT HER PENSION, EVEN THOUGH HER LEGS WERE NO LONGER WHAT THEY WERE, AND ON THE WAY BACK HOME SHE WOULD STOP AT THE OXFAM SHOP AND BUY HERSELF A LITTLE SOMETHING.
OXFAM
Elena's
SEAFOOD BAR
THE OXFAM SHOP SOLD OLD CLOTHES, KNICKNACKS, ODDMENTS, BITS AND BOBS, AND LARGE QUANTITIES OF OLD PAPERBACKS, ALL OF THEM DONATIONS: SECONDHAND FLOTSAM, OFTEN THE HOUSE CLEARANCES OF THE DEAD.
ALL THE PROFITS WENT TO CHARITY.
THE SHOP WAS STAFFED BY VOLUNTEERS. THE VOLUNTEER ON DUTY THIS AFTERNOON WAS MARIE, SEVENTEEN, SLIGHTLY OVERWEIGHT.
HER BAGGY MAUVE JUMPER LOOKED LIKE SHE HAD BOUGHT IT FROM THE SHOP.
MARIE SAT BY THE TILL FILLING OUT A "REVEAL YOUR HIDDEN PERSONALITY" QUESTIONNAIRE.
EVERY NOW AND THEN, SHE'D FLIP TO THE BACK OF THE MAGAZINE AND CHECK THE RELATIVE POINTS ASSIGNED TO AN A), B), OR C) ANSWER BEFORE MAKING UP HER MIND HOW SHE'D RESPOND TO THE QUESTION.

MRS. WHITAKER PUTTERED AROUND THE SHOP

THEY STILL HADN'T SOLD THE STUFFED COBRA, SHE NOTED. IT HAD BEEN THERE FOR SIX MONTHS NOW, GATHERING DUST, GLASS EYES GAZING BALEFULLY AT THE CLOTHES RACKS AND THE CABINET FILLED WITH CHIPPED PORCELAIN AND CHEWED TOYS.

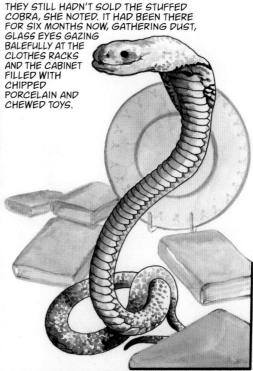

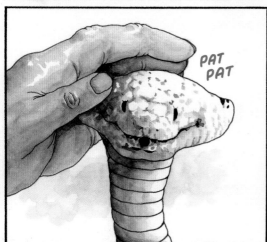

PAT PAT

SHE PICKED OUT A COUPLE OF MILLS AND BOON NOVELS FROM A BOOKSHELF--*HER THUNDERING SOUL* AND *HER TURBULENT HEART*, A SHILLING EACH...

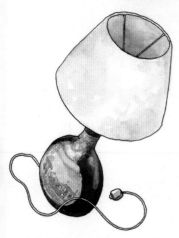

...AND GAVE CAREFUL CONSIDERATION TO THE EMPTY BOTTLE OF MATEUS ROSÉ WITH A DECORATIVE LAMPSHADE ON IT BEFORE DECIDING SHE REALLY DIDN'T HAVE ANYWHERE TO PUT IT.

SHE MOVED A RATHER THREADBARE FUR COAT, WHICH SMELLED BADLY OF MOTHBALLS.

UNDERNEATH WAS A WALKING STICK AND A WATER-STAINED COPY OF *ROMANCE AND LEGEND OF CHIVALRY* BY A.R. HOPE MONCRIEFF, PRICED AT FIVE PENCE.

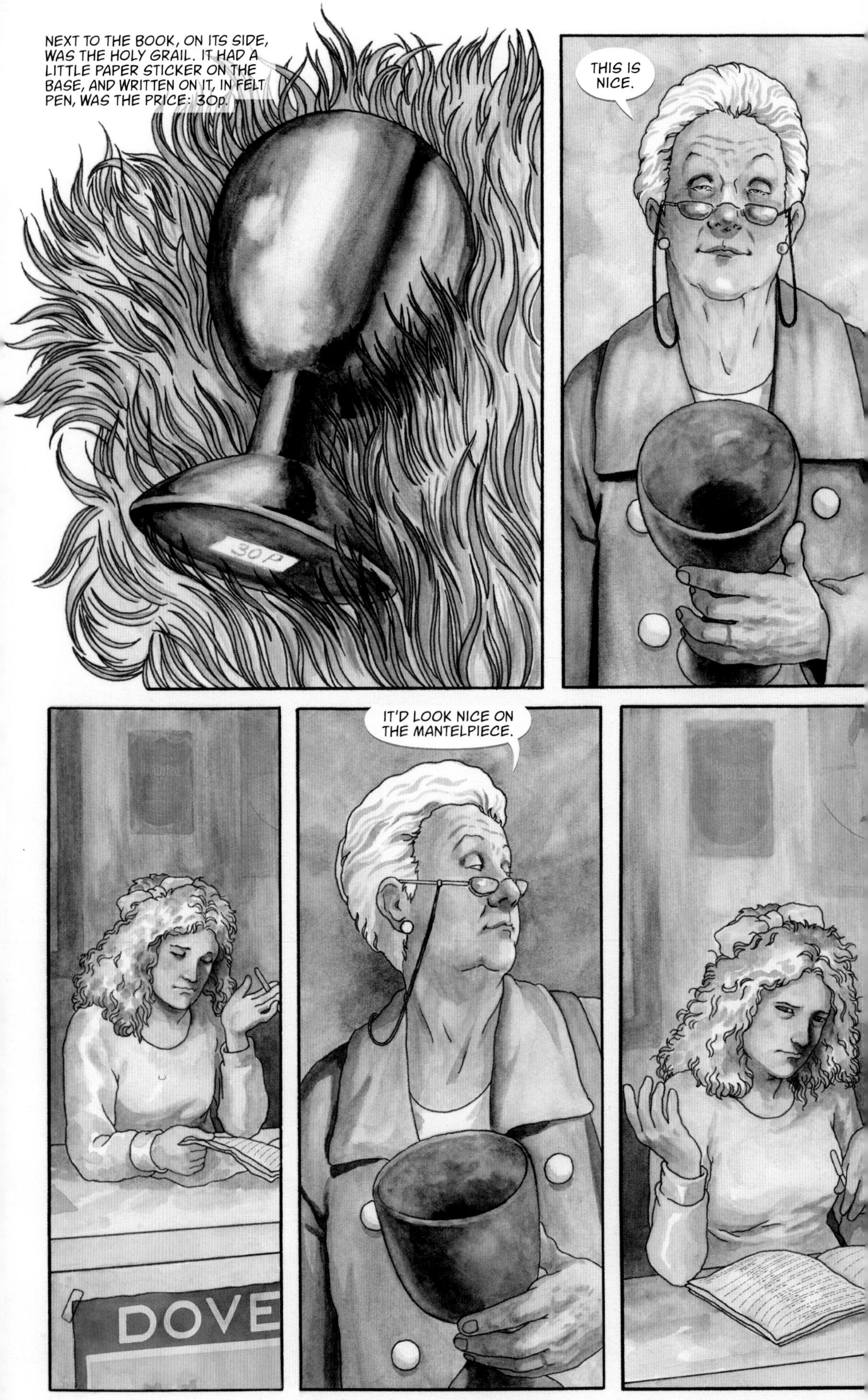
NEXT TO THE BOOK, ON ITS SIDE, WAS THE HOLY GRAIL. IT HAD A LITTLE PAPER STICKER ON THE BASE, AND WRITTEN ON IT, IN FELT PEN, WAS THE PRICE: 30p.
30p
THIS IS NICE.
IT'D LOOK NICE ON THE MANTELPIECE.
DOVE

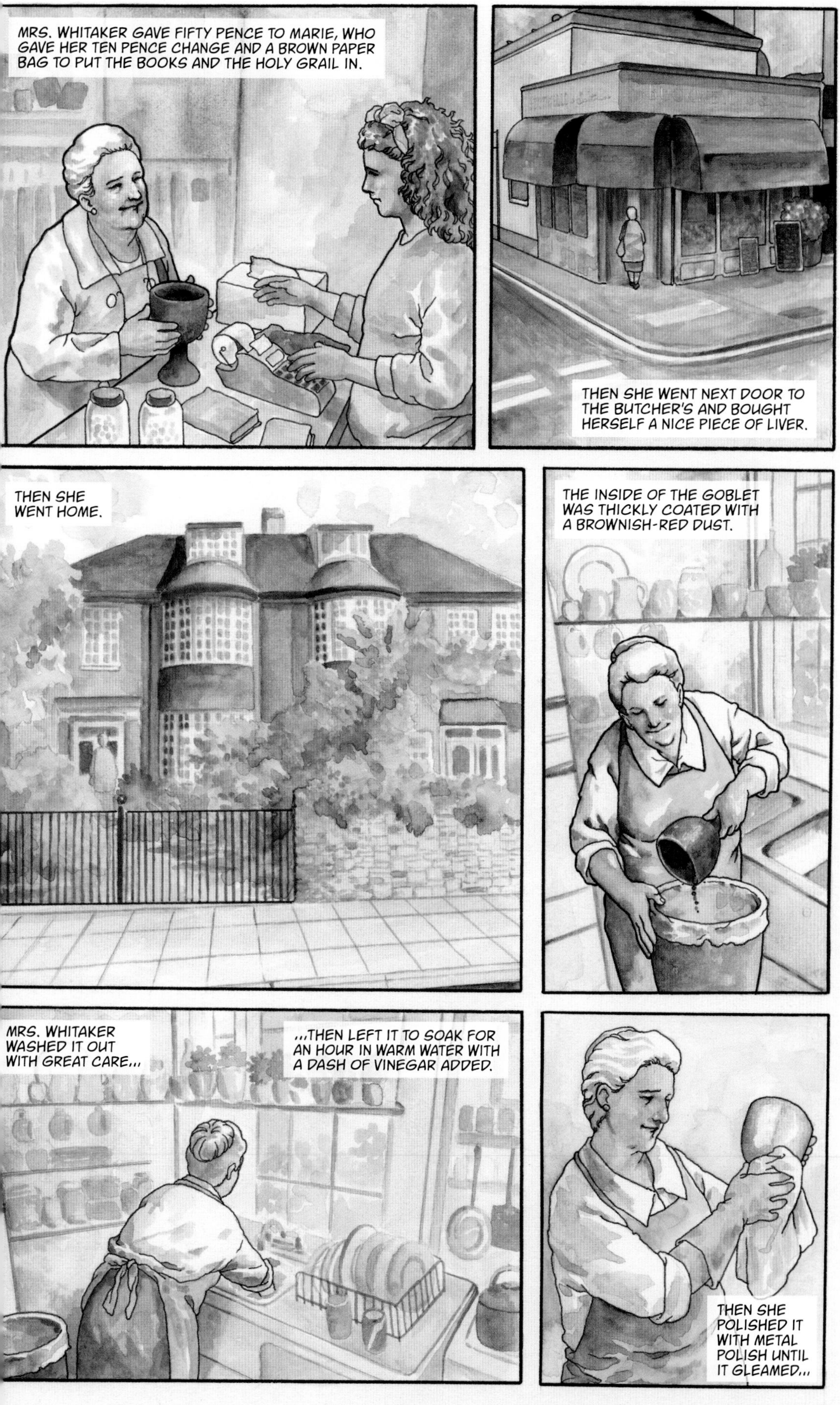
MRS. WHITAKER GAVE FIFTY PENCE TO MARIE, WHO GAVE HER TEN PENCE CHANGE AND A BROWN PAPER BAG TO PUT THE BOOKS AND THE HOLY GRAIL IN.
THEN SHE WENT NEXT DOOR TO THE BUTCHER'S AND BOUGHT HERSELF A NICE PIECE OF LIVER.
THEN SHE WENT HOME.
THE INSIDE OF THE GOBLET WAS THICKLY COATED WITH A BROWNISH-RED DUST.
MRS. WHITAKER WASHED IT OUT WITH GREAT CARE...
...THEN LEFT IT TO SOAK FOR AN HOUR IN WARM WATER WITH A DASH OF VINEGAR ADDED.
THEN SHE POLISHED IT WITH METAL POLISH UNTIL IT GLEAMED...

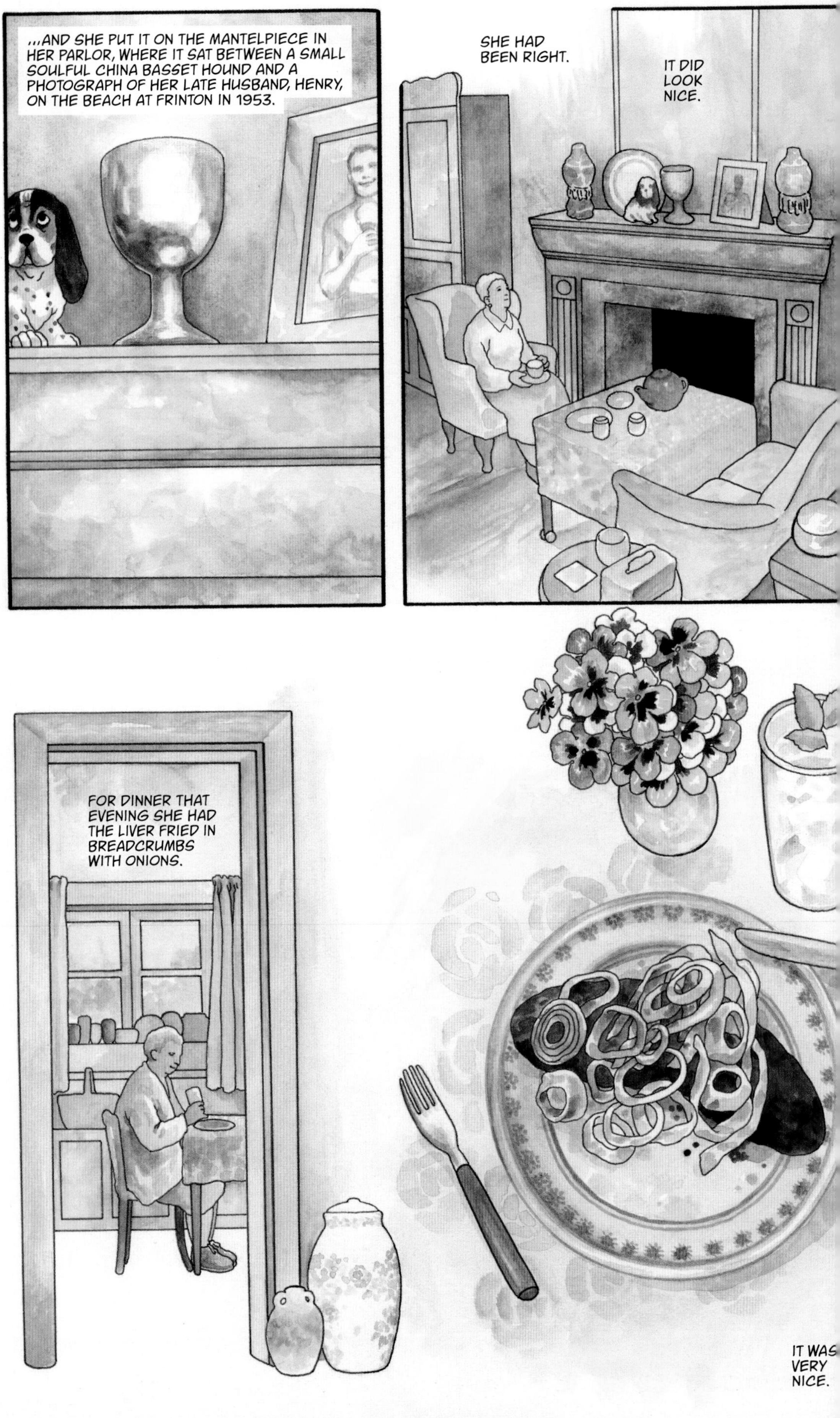
...AND SHE PUT IT ON THE MANTELPIECE IN HER PARLOR, WHERE IT SAT BETWEEN A SMALL SOULFUL CHINA BASSET HOUND AND A PHOTOGRAPH OF HER LATE HUSBAND, HENRY, ON THE BEACH AT FRINTON IN 1953.
SHE HAD BEEN RIGHT.
IT DID LOOK NICE.
FOR DINNER THAT EVENING SHE HAD THE LIVER FRIED IN BREADCRUMBS WITH ONIONS.
IT WAS VERY NICE.

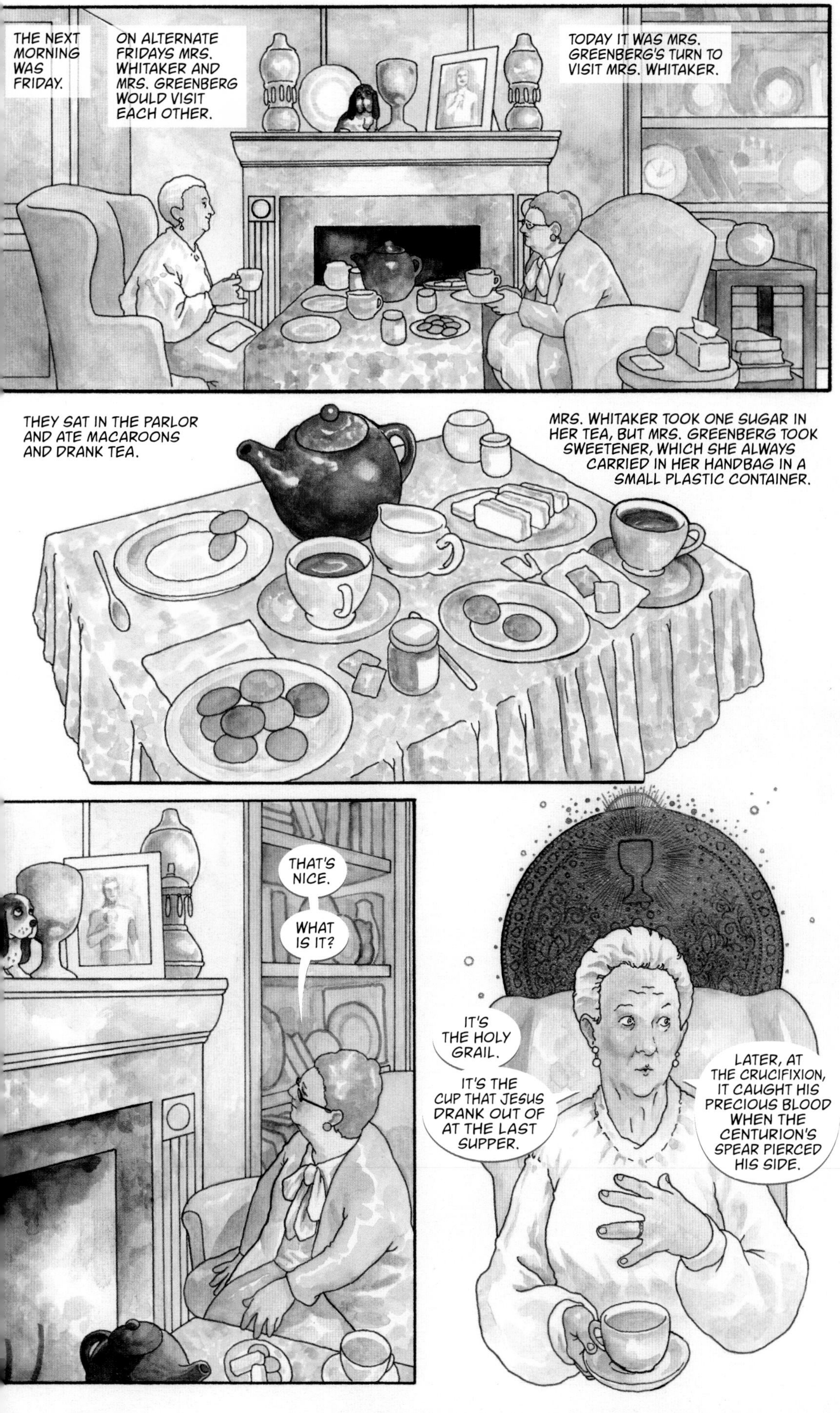

THE NEXT MORNING WAS FRIDAY.
ON ALTERNATE FRIDAYS MRS. WHITAKER AND MRS. GREENBERG WOULD VISIT EACH OTHER.
TODAY IT WAS MRS. GREENBERG'S TURN TO VISIT MRS. WHITAKER.
THEY SAT IN THE PARLOR AND ATE MACAROONS AND DRANK TEA.
MRS. WHITAKER TOOK ONE SUGAR IN HER TEA, BUT MRS. GREENBERG TOOK SWEETENER, WHICH SHE ALWAYS CARRIED IN HER HANDBAG IN A SMALL PLASTIC CONTAINER.
THAT'S NICE.
WHAT IS IT?
IT'S THE HOLY GRAIL.
IT'S THE CUP THAT JESUS DRANK OUT OF AT THE LAST SUPPER.
LATER, AT THE CRUCIFIXION, IT CAUGHT HIS PRECIOUS BLOOD WHEN THE CENTURION'S SPEAR PIERCED HIS SIDE.

SNIFF!

I WOULDN'T KNOW ABOUT THAT, BUT IT'S VERY NICE.

OUR MYRON GOT ONE JUST LIKE THAT WHEN HE WON THE SWIMMING TOURNAMENT, ONLY IT'S GOT HIS NAME ON THE SIDE.

IS HE STILL WITH THAT NICE GIRL? THE HAIRDRESSER?

BERNICE? OH YES. THEY'RE THINKING OF GETTING ENGAGED.

THAT'S NICE.

MRS. WHITAKER TOOK ANOTHER MACAROON.

MRS. GREENBERG BAKED HER OWN MACAROONS AND BROUGHT THEM OVER EVERY ALTERNATE FRIDAY,,,

...SMALL SWEET LIGHT BROWN BISCUITS WITH ALMONDS ON TOP.

THEY TALKED ABOUT MYRON AND BERNICE, AND MRS. WHITAKER'S NEPHEW RONALD (SHE HAD HAD NO CHILDREN).

AND ABOUT THEIR FRIEND MRS. PERKINS WHO WAS IN HOSPITAL WITH HER HIP, POOR DEAR.

AT MIDDAY MRS. GREENBERG WENT HOME, AND MRS. WHITAKER MADE HERSELF CHEESE ON TOAST FOR LUNCH.

AFTER LUNCH MRS. WHITAKER TOOK HER PILLS; THE WHITE AND THE RED AND TWO LITTLE ORANGE ONES.

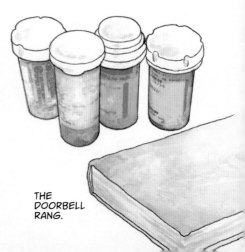

THE DOORBELL RANG.

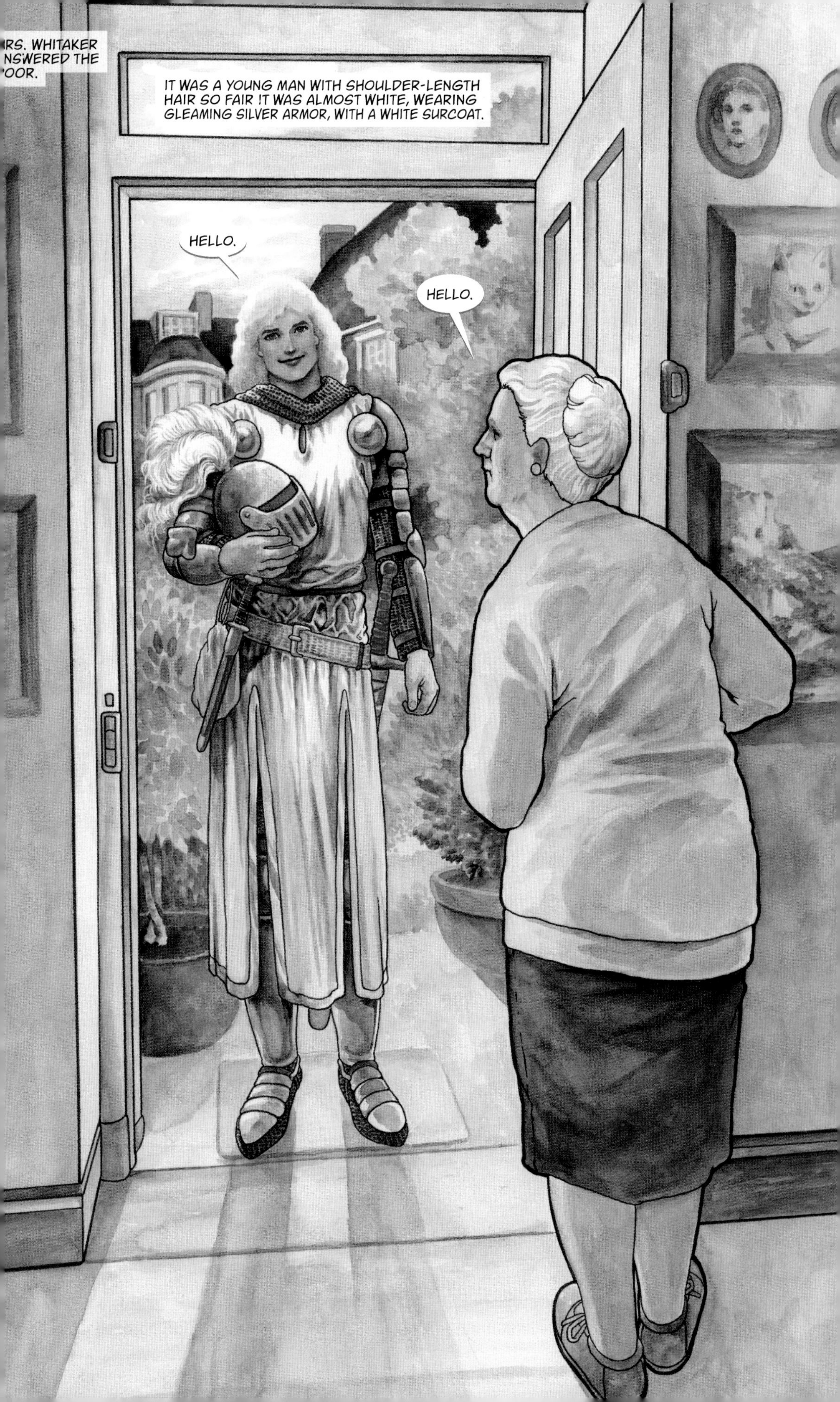
RS. WHITAKER
NSWERED THE
OOR.
IT WAS A YOUNG MAN WITH SHOULDER-LENGTH HAIR SO FAIR IT WAS ALMOST WHITE, WEARING GLEAMING SILVER ARMOR, WITH A WHITE SURCOAT.
HELLO.
HELLO.

I'M ON A QUEST.

THAT'S NICE.

CAN I COME IN?

I'M SORRY. I DON'T THINK SO.

I'M ON A QUEST FOR THE HOLY GRAIL.

IS IT HERE?

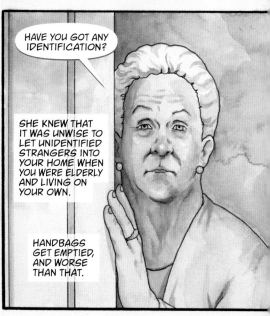

HAVE YOU GOT ANY IDENTIFICATION?

SHE KNEW THAT IT WAS UNWISE TO LET UNIDENTIFIED STRANGERS INTO YOUR HOME WHEN YOU WERE ELDERLY AND LIVING ON YOUR OWN.

HANDBAGS GET EMPTIED, AND WORSE THAN THAT.

THE YOUNG MAN WENT BACK DOWN THE GARDEN PATH. HIS HORSE, A HUGE GRAY CHARGER, BIG AS A SHIRE-HORSE, ITS HEAD HIGH AND ITS EYES INTELLIGENT, WAS TETHERED TO MRS. WHITAKER'S GARDEN GATE.

THE KNIGHT FUMBLED IN THE SADDLEBAG AND RETURNED WITH A SCROLL.

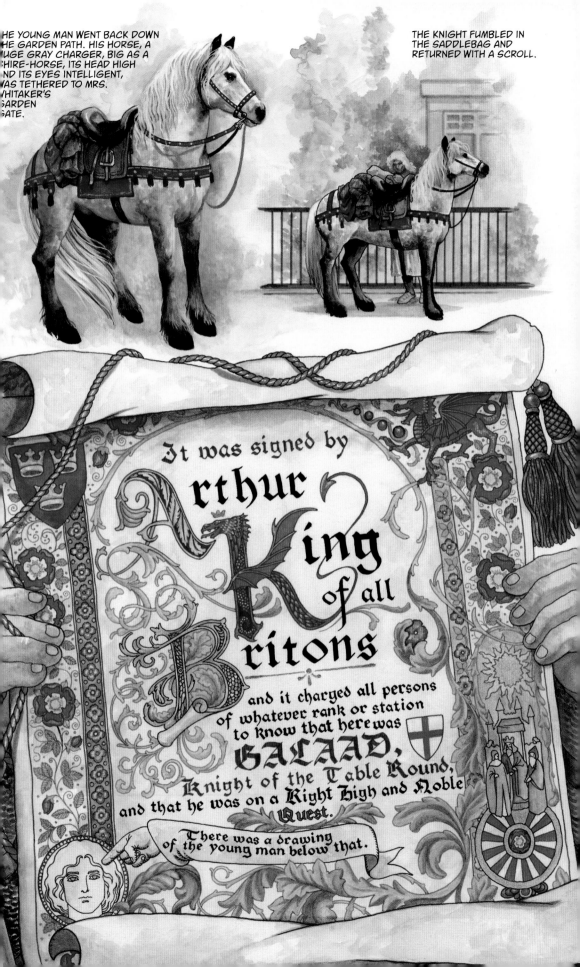

It was signed by **Arthur King of all Britons**

and it charged all persons of whatever rank or station to know that here was **GALAAD,** Knight of the Table Round, and that he was on a Right High and Noble Quest.

There was a drawing of the young man below that.

IT WASN'T A
BAD LIKENESS.

MRS. WHITAKER HAD BEEN
EXPECTING A LITTLE CARD
WITH A PHOTOGRAPH ON IT,
BUT THIS WAS FAR MORE
IMPRESSIVE.

I
SUPPOSE
YOU HAD
BETTER
COME
IN.

THEY WENT INTO HER KITCHEN.

SHE MADE GALAAD
A CUP OF TEA, THEN
SHE TOOK HIM INTO
THE PARLOR.

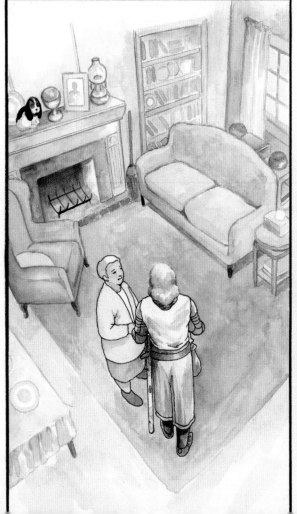

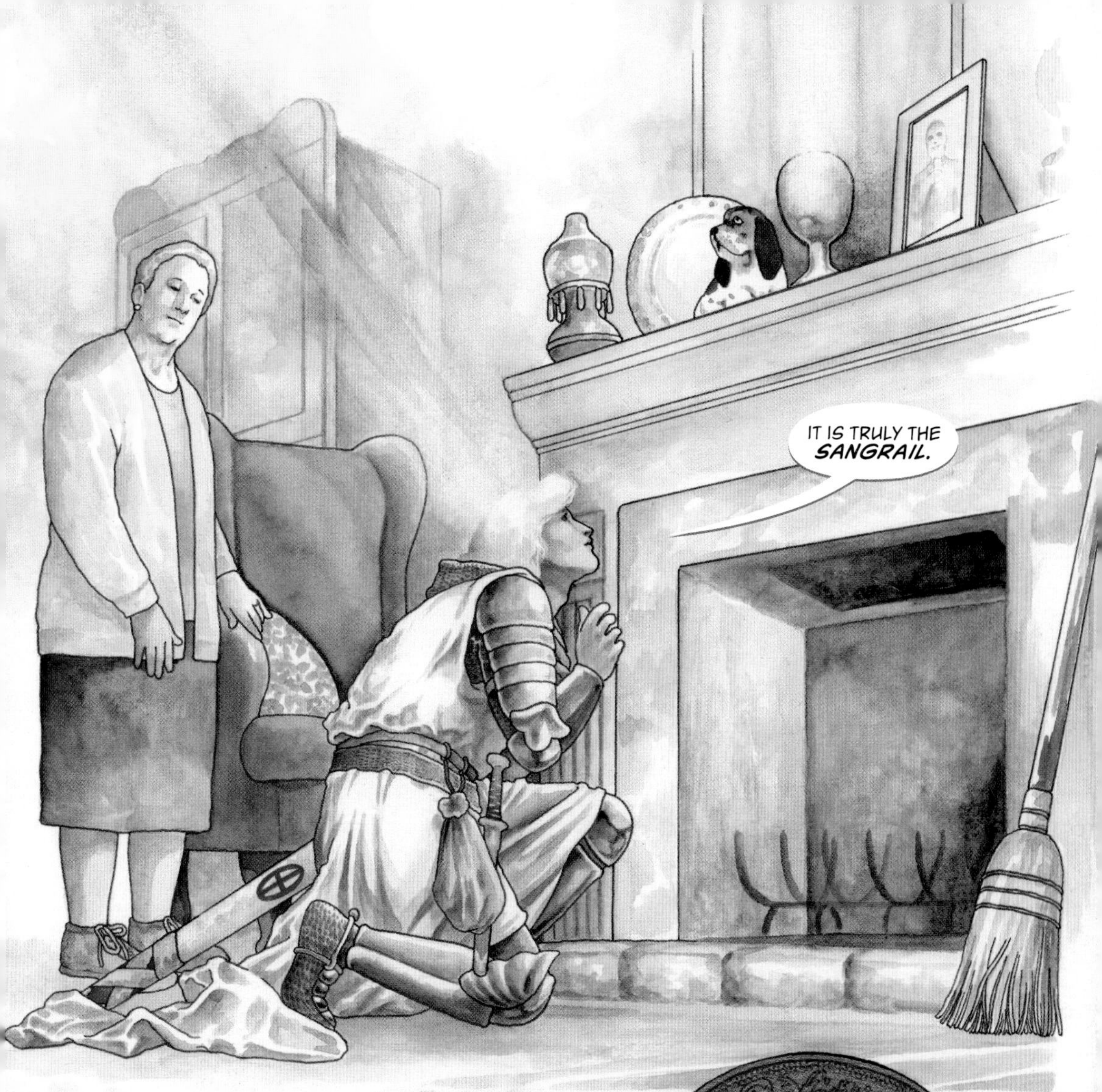
IT IS TRULY THE SANGRAIL.

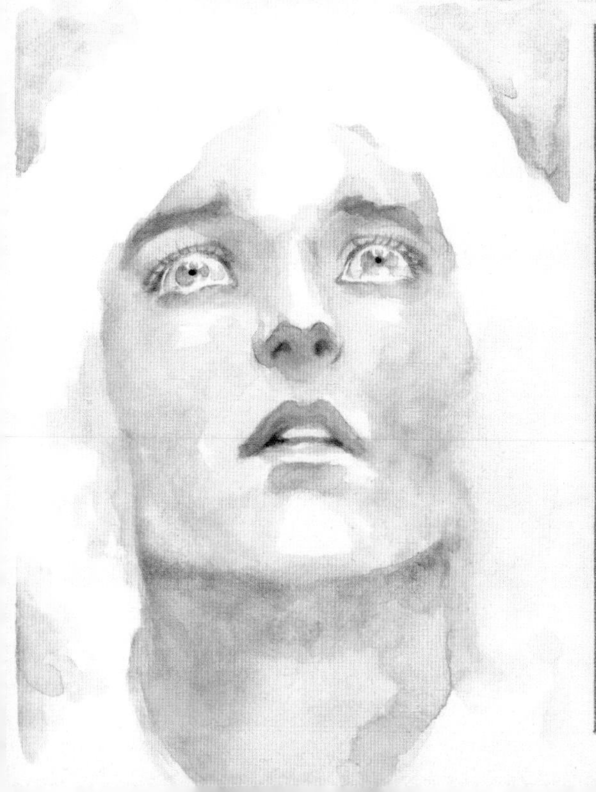

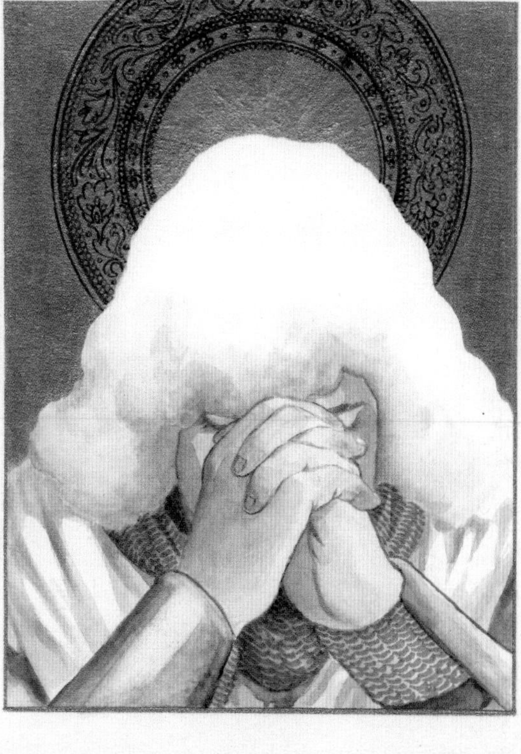

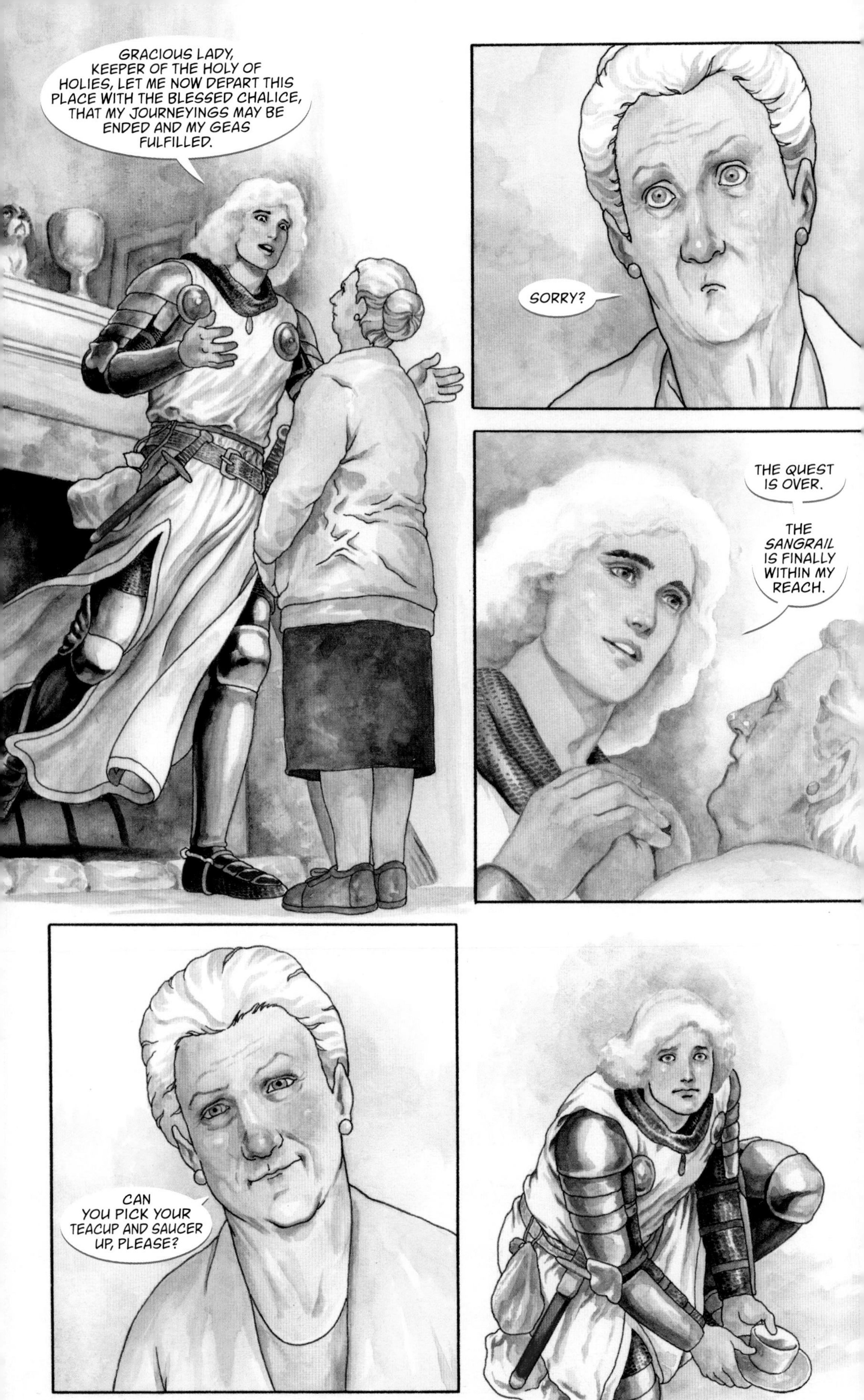
GRACIOUS LADY, KEEPER OF THE HOLY OF HOLIES, LET ME NOW DEPART THIS PLACE WITH THE BLESSED CHALICE, THAT MY JOURNEYINGS MAY BE ENDED AND MY GEAS FULFILLED.
SORRY?
THE QUEST IS OVER.
THE *SANGRAIL* IS FINALLY WITHIN MY REACH.
CAN YOU PICK YOUR TEACUP AND SAUCER UP, PLEASE?

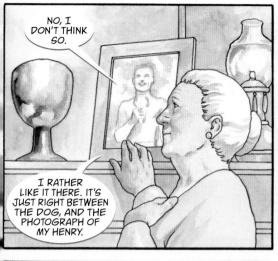

NO, I DON'T THINK SO.

I RATHER LIKE IT THERE. IT'S JUST RIGHT BETWEEN THE DOG, AND THE PHOTOGRAPH OF MY HENRY.

IS IT GOLD YOU NEED? IS THAT IT?

LADY, I CAN BRING YOU GOLD...

NO, I DON'T WANT ANY GOLD, THANK YOU.

I'M SIMPLY NOT INTERESTED.

SHE USHERED GALAAD TO THE FRONT DOOR.

NICE TO MEET YOU.

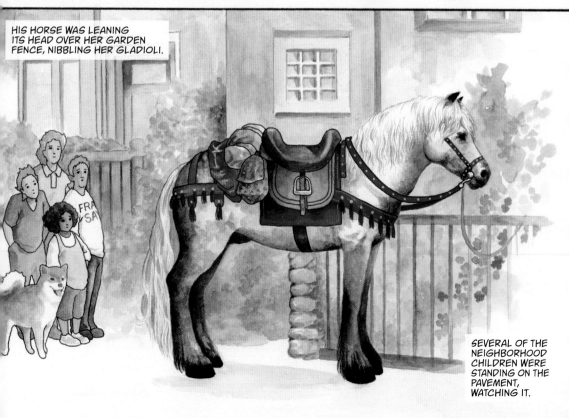

HIS HORSE WAS LEANING ITS HEAD OVER HER GARDEN FENCE, NIBBLING HER GLADIOLI.

SEVERAL OF THE NEIGHBORHOOD CHILDREN WERE STANDING ON THE PAVEMENT, WATCHING IT.

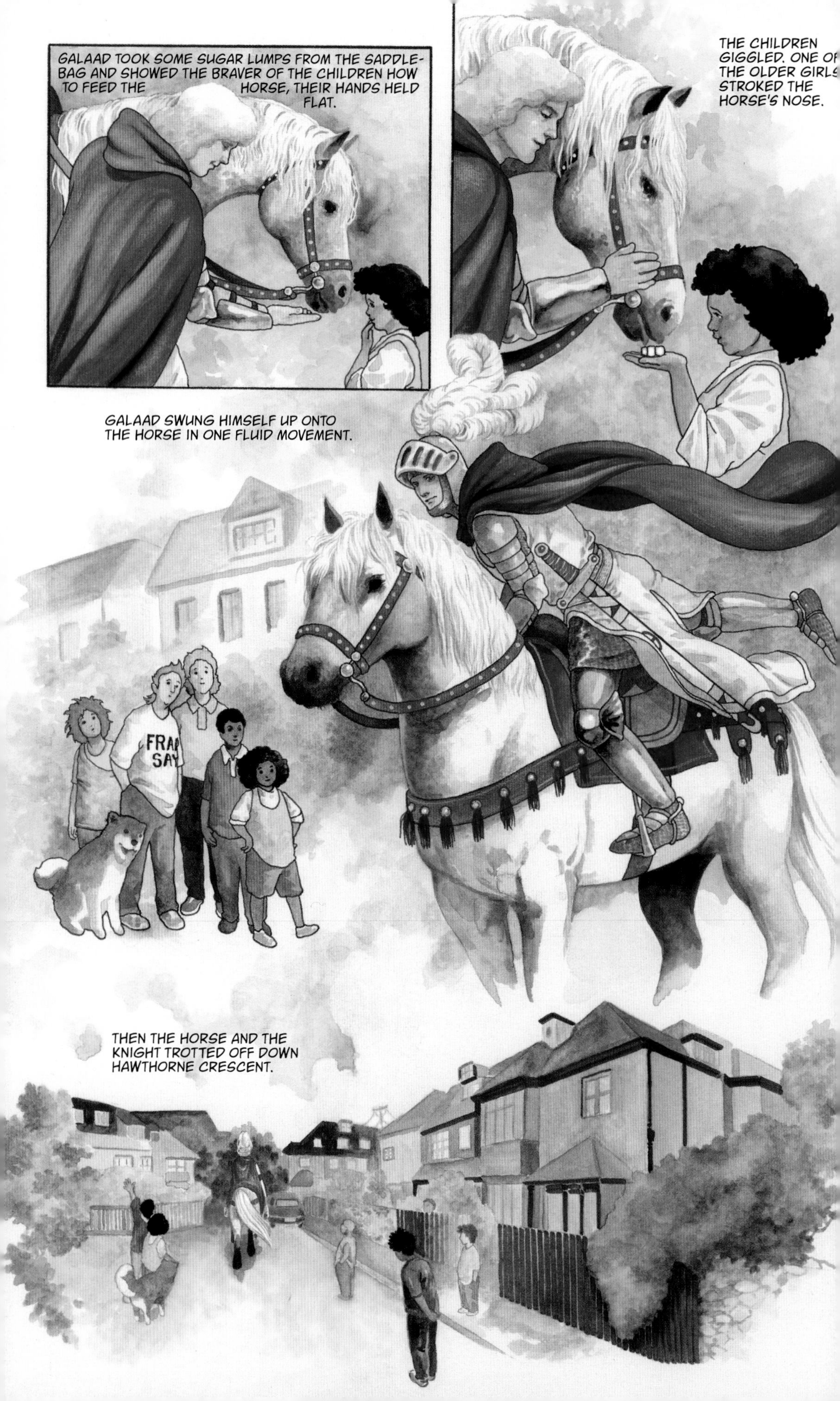
GALAAD TOOK SOME SUGAR LUMPS FROM THE SADDLE-BAG AND SHOWED THE BRAVER OF THE CHILDREN HOW TO FEED THE HORSE, THEIR HANDS HELD FLAT.
THE CHILDREN GIGGLED. ONE OF THE OLDER GIRLS STROKED THE HORSE'S NOSE.
GALAAD SWUNG HIMSELF UP ONTO THE HORSE IN ONE FLUID MOVEMENT.
THEN THE HORSE AND THE KNIGHT TROTTED OFF DOWN HAWTHORNE CRESCENT.

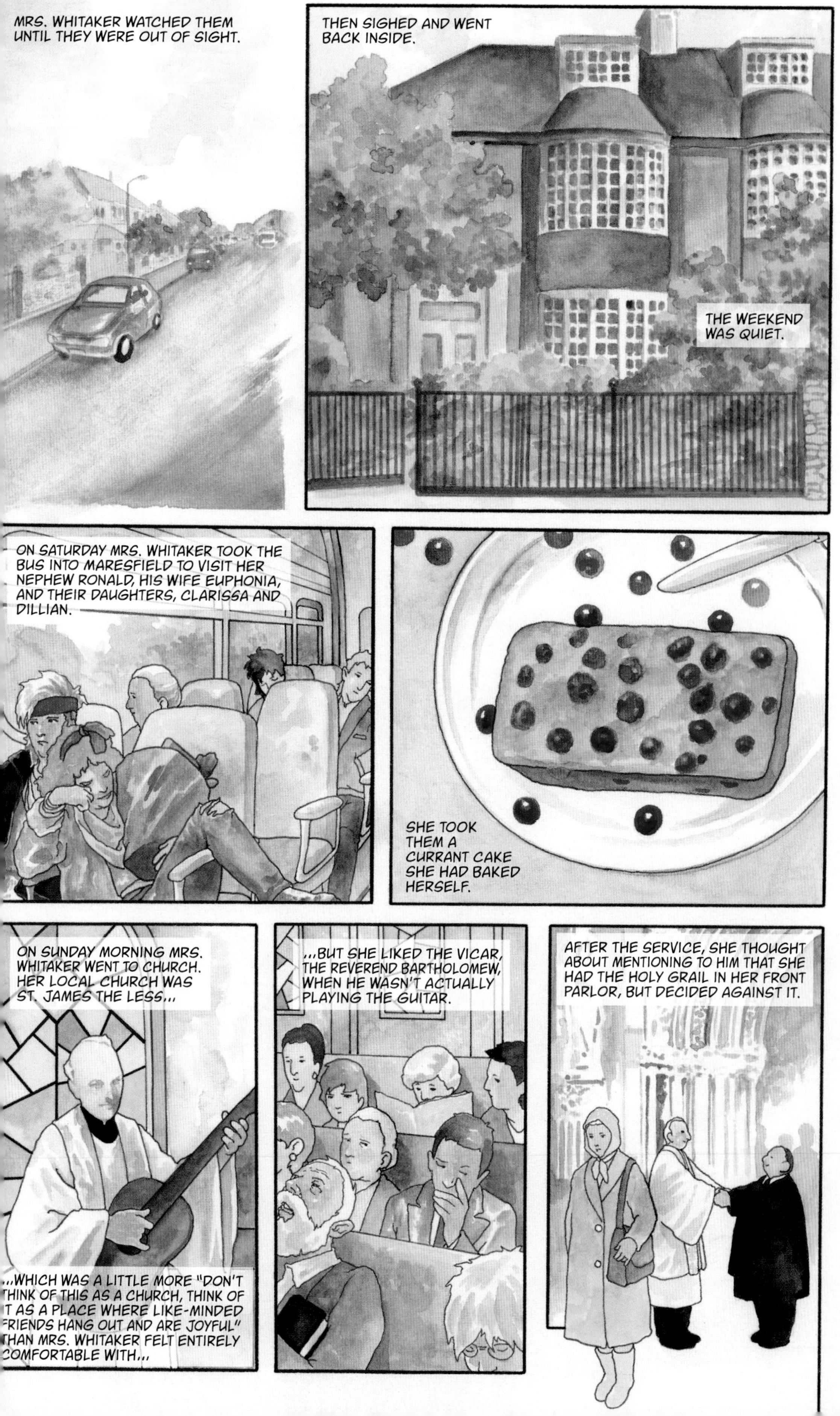

MRS. WHITAKER WATCHED THEM UNTIL THEY WERE OUT OF SIGHT.
THEN SIGHED AND WENT BACK INSIDE.
THE WEEKEND WAS QUIET.
ON SATURDAY MRS. WHITAKER TOOK THE BUS INTO MARESFIELD TO VISIT HER NEPHEW RONALD, HIS WIFE EUPHONIA, AND THEIR DAUGHTERS, CLARISSA AND DILLIAN.
SHE TOOK THEM A CURRANT CAKE SHE HAD BAKED HERSELF.
ON SUNDAY MORNING MRS. WHITAKER WENT TO CHURCH. HER LOCAL CHURCH WAS ST. JAMES THE LESS...
...WHICH WAS A LITTLE MORE "DON'T THINK OF THIS AS A CHURCH, THINK OF IT AS A PLACE WHERE LIKE-MINDED FRIENDS HANG OUT AND ARE JOYFUL" THAN MRS. WHITAKER FELT ENTIRELY COMFORTABLE WITH...
...BUT SHE LIKED THE VICAR, THE REVEREND BARTHOLOMEW, WHEN HE WASN'T ACTUALLY PLAYING THE GUITAR.
AFTER THE SERVICE, SHE THOUGHT ABOUT MENTIONING TO HIM THAT SHE HAD THE HOLY GRAIL IN HER FRONT PARLOR, BUT DECIDED AGAINST IT.

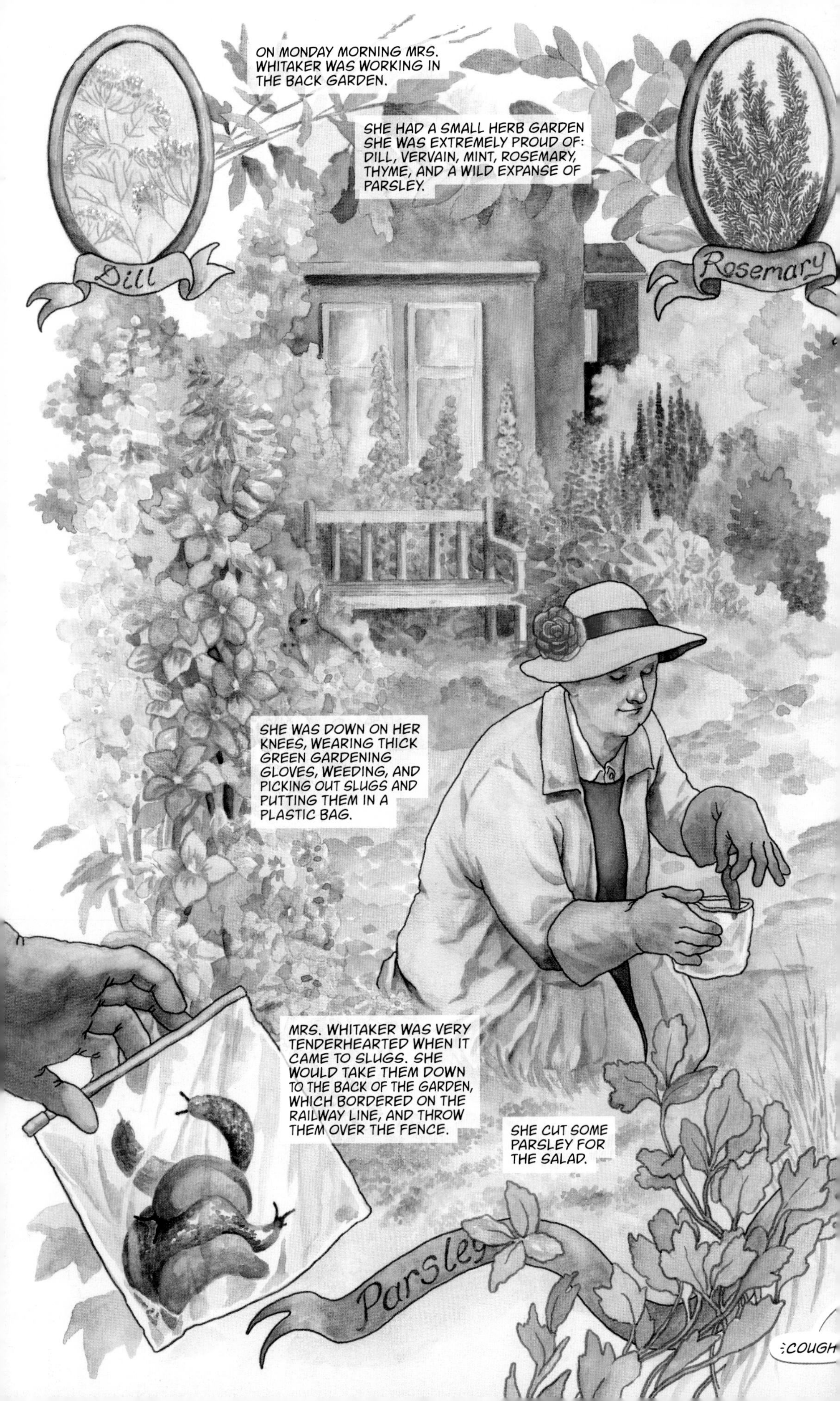

ON MONDAY MORNING MRS. WHITAKER WAS WORKING IN THE BACK GARDEN.
SHE HAD A SMALL HERB GARDEN SHE WAS EXTREMELY PROUD OF: DILL, VERVAIN, MINT, ROSEMARY, THYME, AND A WILD EXPANSE OF PARSLEY.
Dill
Rosemary
SHE WAS DOWN ON HER KNEES, WEARING THICK GREEN GARDENING GLOVES, WEEDING, AND PICKING OUT SLUGS AND PUTTING THEM IN A PLASTIC BAG.
MRS. WHITAKER WAS VERY TENDERHEARTED WHEN IT CAME TO SLUGS. SHE WOULD TAKE THEM DOWN TO THE BACK OF THE GARDEN, WHICH BORDERED ON THE RAILWAY LINE, AND THROW THEM OVER THE FENCE.
SHE CUT SOME PARSLEY FOR THE SALAD.
Parsley
:COUGH

GALAHAD STOOD THERE, TALL AND BEAUTIFUL, HIS ARMOR GLINTING IN THE MORNING SUN.

IN HIS ARMS HE HELD A LONG PACKAGE, WRAPPED IN OILED LEATHER.

I'M BACK.

HELLO.

WELL, NOW YOU'RE HERE, YOU MIGHT AS WELL MAKE YOURSELF USEFUL.

SHE GAVE HIM THE PLASTIC BAG FULL OF SLUGS AND TOLD HIM TO TIP THE SLUGS OUT OVER THE BACK OF THE FENCE.

HE DID.

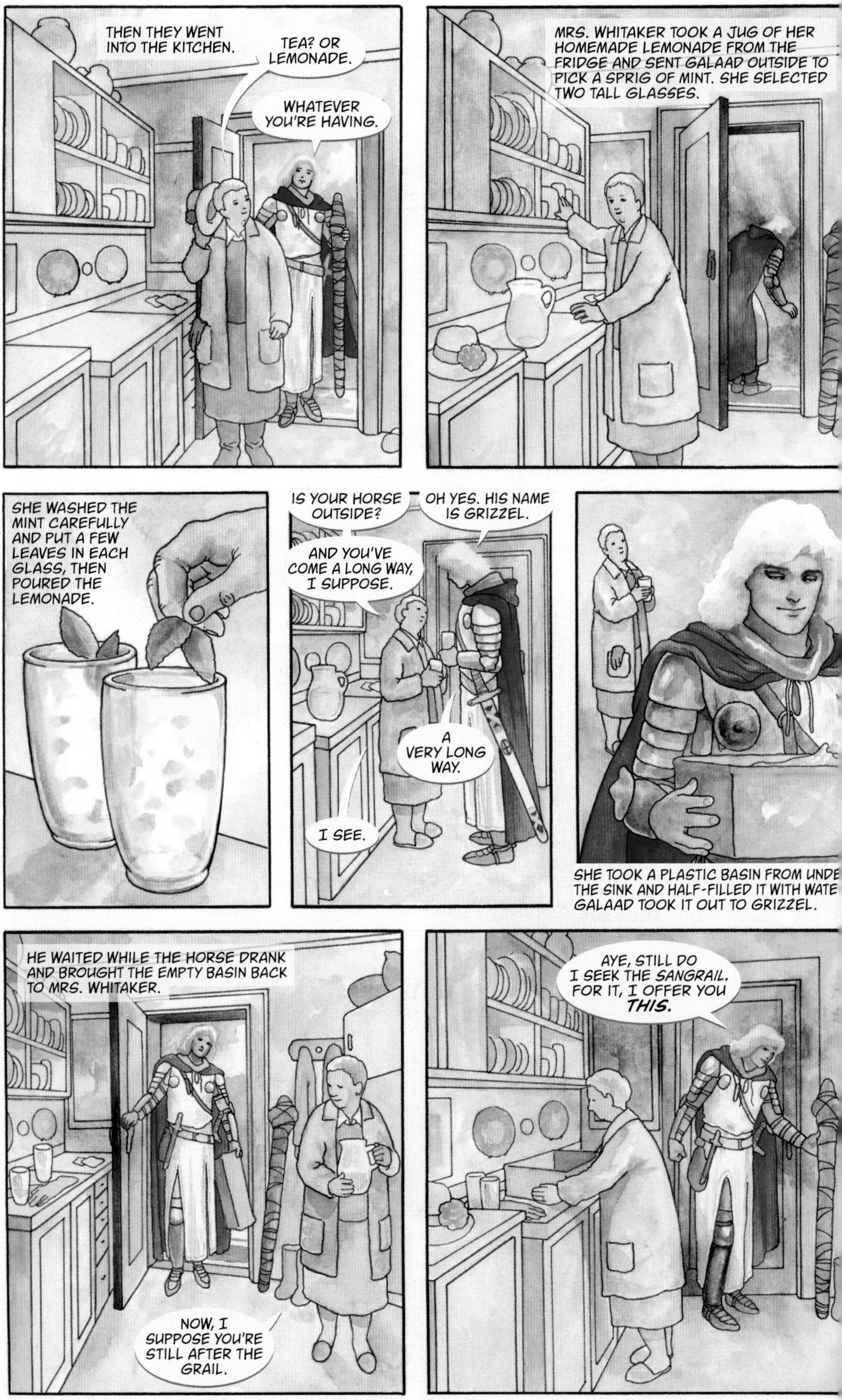
THEN THEY WENT INTO THE KITCHEN.
TEA? OR LEMONADE.
WHATEVER YOU'RE HAVING.
MRS. WHITAKER TOOK A JUG OF HER HOMEMADE LEMONADE FROM THE FRIDGE AND SENT GALAAD OUTSIDE TO PICK A SPRIG OF MINT. SHE SELECTED TWO TALL GLASSES.
SHE WASHED THE MINT CAREFULLY AND PUT A FEW LEAVES IN EACH GLASS, THEN POURED THE LEMONADE.
IS YOUR HORSE OUTSIDE?
OH YES. HIS NAME IS GRIZZEL.
AND YOU'VE COME A LONG WAY, I SUPPOSE.
A VERY LONG WAY.
I SEE.
SHE TOOK A PLASTIC BASIN FROM UNDE THE SINK AND HALF-FILLED IT WITH WATE GALAAD TOOK IT OUT TO GRIZZEL.
HE WAITED WHILE THE HORSE DRANK AND BROUGHT THE EMPTY BASIN BACK TO MRS. WHITAKER.
NOW, I SUPPOSE YOU'RE STILL AFTER THE GRAIL.
AYE, STILL DO I SEEK THE *SANGRAIL*. FOR IT, I OFFER YOU ***THIS.***

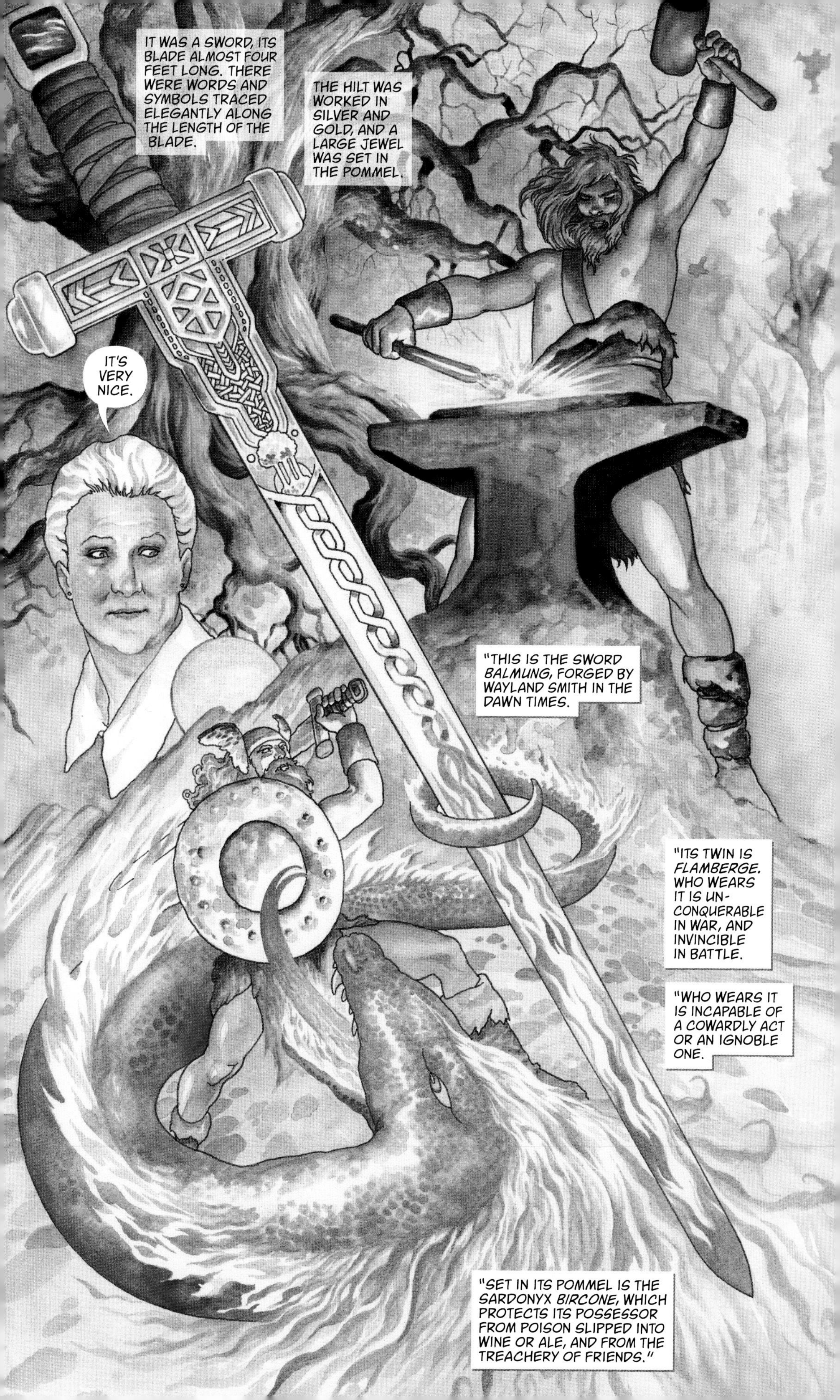
IT WAS A SWORD, ITS BLADE ALMOST FOUR FEET LONG. THERE WERE WORDS AND SYMBOLS TRACED ELEGANTLY ALONG THE LENGTH OF THE BLADE.
THE HILT WAS WORKED IN SILVER AND GOLD, AND A LARGE JEWEL WAS SET IN THE POMMEL.
IT'S VERY NICE.
"THIS IS THE SWORD *BALMUNG*, FORGED BY WAYLAND SMITH IN THE DAWN TIMES.
"ITS TWIN IS *FLAMBERGE*. WHO WEARS IT IS UN-CONQUERABLE IN WAR, AND INVINCIBLE IN BATTLE.
"WHO WEARS IT IS INCAPABLE OF A COWARDLY ACT OR AN IGNOBLE ONE.
"SET IN ITS POMMEL IS THE SARDONYX *BIRCONE*, WHICH PROTECTS ITS POSSESSOR FROM POISON SLIPPED INTO WINE OR ALE, AND FROM THE TREACHERY OF FRIENDS."

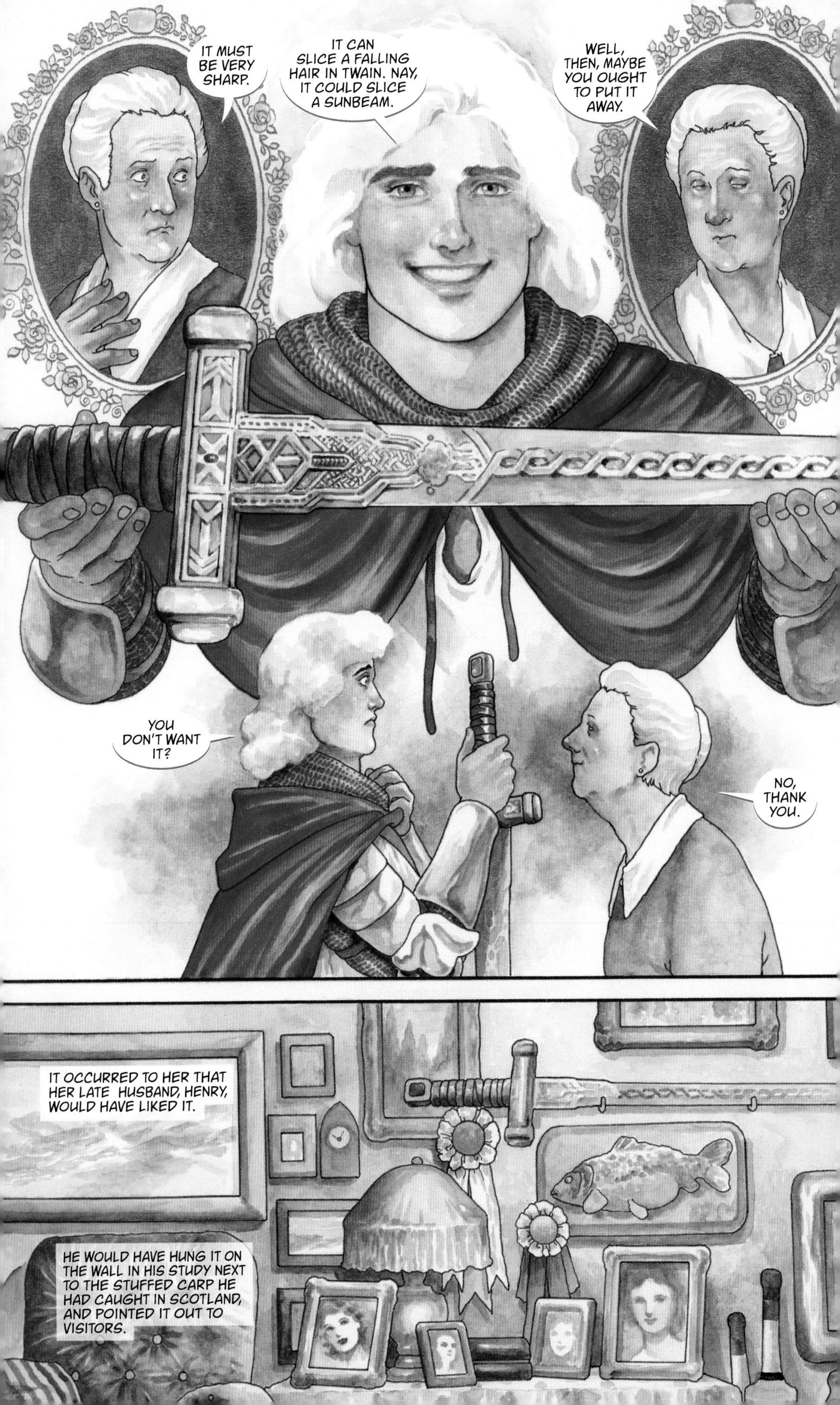
IT MUST BE VERY SHARP.
IT CAN SLICE A FALLING HAIR IN TWAIN. NAY, IT COULD SLICE A SUNBEAM.
WELL, THEN, MAYBE YOU OUGHT TO PUT IT AWAY.
YOU DON'T WANT IT?
NO, THANK YOU.
IT OCCURRED TO HER THAT HER LATE HUSBAND, HENRY, WOULD HAVE LIKED IT.
HE WOULD HAVE HUNG IT ON THE WALL IN HIS STUDY NEXT TO THE STUFFED CARP HE HAD CAUGHT IN SCOTLAND, AND POINTED IT OUT TO VISITORS.

GALAAD REWRAPPED THE OILED LEATHER AROUND THE SWORD BALMUNG AND TIED IT UP WITH WHITE CORD.

HE SAT THERE, DISCONSOLATE.

MRS. WHITAKER MADE HIM SOME CREAM CHEESE AND CUCUMBER SANDWICHES FOR THE JOURNEY BACK AND WRAPPED THEM IN GREASEPROOF PAPER.

SHE GAVE HIM AN APPLE FOR GRIZZEL. HE SEEMED VERY PLEASED WITH BOTH GIFTS.

SHE WAVED THEM GOOD-BYE.

THAT AFTERNOON SHE TOOK THE BUS DOWN TO THE HOSPITAL TO SEE MRS. PERKINS, WHO WAS STILL IN WITH HER HIP, POOR LOVE.

MRS. WHITAKER TOOK HER SOME HOMEMADE FRUITCAKE, ALTHOUGH SHE HAD LEFT OUT THE WALNUTS FROM THE RECIPE, BECAUSE MRS. PERKINS'S TEETH WEREN'T WHAT THEY USED TO BE.

SHE WATCHED A LITTLE TELEVISION THAT EVENING, AND HAD AN EARLY NIGHT.

ON TUESDAY THE POSTMAN CALLED.

MRS. WHITAKER WAS UP IN THE BOXROOM AT THE TOP OF THE HOUSE, DOING A SPOT OF TIDYING, AND, TAKING EACH STEP SLOWLY AND CAREFULLY, SHE DIDN'T MAKE IT DOWNSTAIRS IN TIME.

THE POSTMAN HAD LEFT HER A MESSAGE WHICH SAID THAT HE'D TRIED TO DELIVER A PACKET, BUT NO ONE WAS HOME.

:SIGH:

SHE PUT THE MESSAGE INTO HER HANDBAG AND WENT DOWN TO THE POST OFFICE.

DISTINCTION

THE PACKAGE WAS FROM HER NIECE SHIRELLE IN SYDNEY, AUSTRALIA.

IT CONTAINED PHOTOGRAPHS OF HER HUSBAND, WALLACE, AND HER TWO DAUGHTERS, DIXIE AND VIOLET, AND A CONCH SHELL PACKED IN COTTON WOOL.

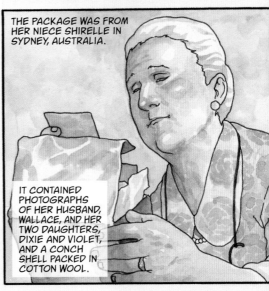

MRS. WHITAKER HAD A NUMBER OF ORNAMENTAL SHELLS IN HER BEDROOM. HER FAVORITE HAD A VIEW OF THE BAHAMAS DONE ON IT IN ENAMEL.

IT HAD BEEN A GIFT FROM HER SISTER, ETHEL, WHO HAD DIED IN 1983.

SHE PUT THE SHELL AND THE PHOTOGRAPHS IN HER SHOPPING BAG. THEN, SEEING THAT SHE WAS IN THE AREA, SHE STOPPED IN AT THE OXFAM SHOP ON HER WAY HOME.

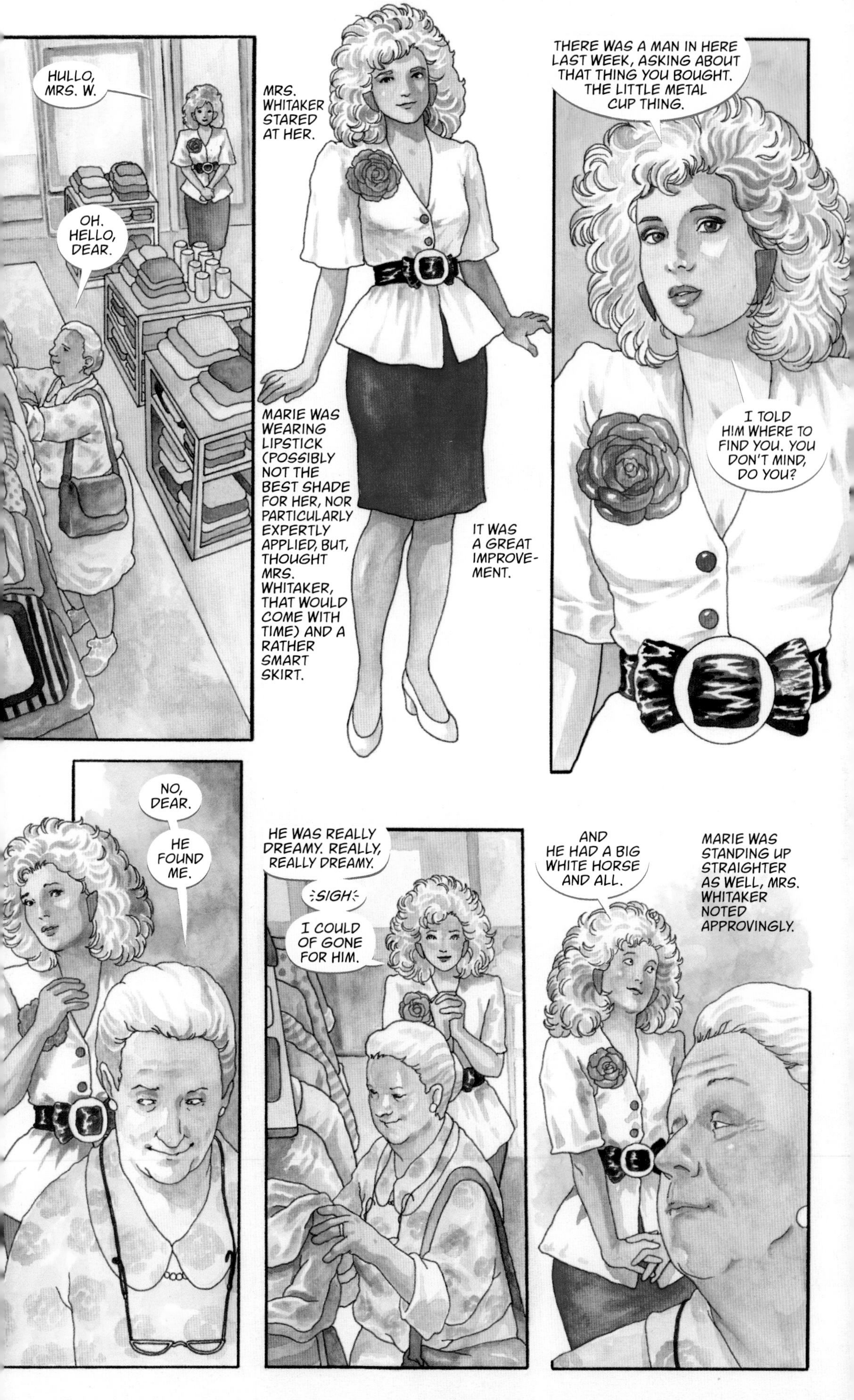
HULLO, MRS. W.
OH. HELLO, DEAR.
MRS. WHITAKER STARED AT HER.
MARIE WAS WEARING LIPSTICK (POSSIBLY NOT THE BEST SHADE FOR HER, NOR PARTICULARLY EXPERTLY APPLIED, BUT, THOUGHT MRS. WHITAKER, THAT WOULD COME WITH TIME) AND A RATHER SMART SKIRT.
IT WAS A GREAT IMPROVE-MENT.
THERE WAS A MAN IN HERE LAST WEEK, ASKING ABOUT THAT THING YOU BOUGHT. THE LITTLE METAL CUP THING.
I TOLD HIM WHERE TO FIND YOU. YOU DON'T MIND, DO YOU?
NO, DEAR.
HE FOUND ME.
HE WAS REALLY DREAMY. REALLY, REALLY DREAMY.
SIGH
I COULD OF GONE FOR HIM.
AND HE HAD A BIG WHITE HORSE AND ALL.
MARIE WAS STANDING UP STRAIGHTER AS WELL, MRS. WHITAKER NOTED APPROVINGLY.

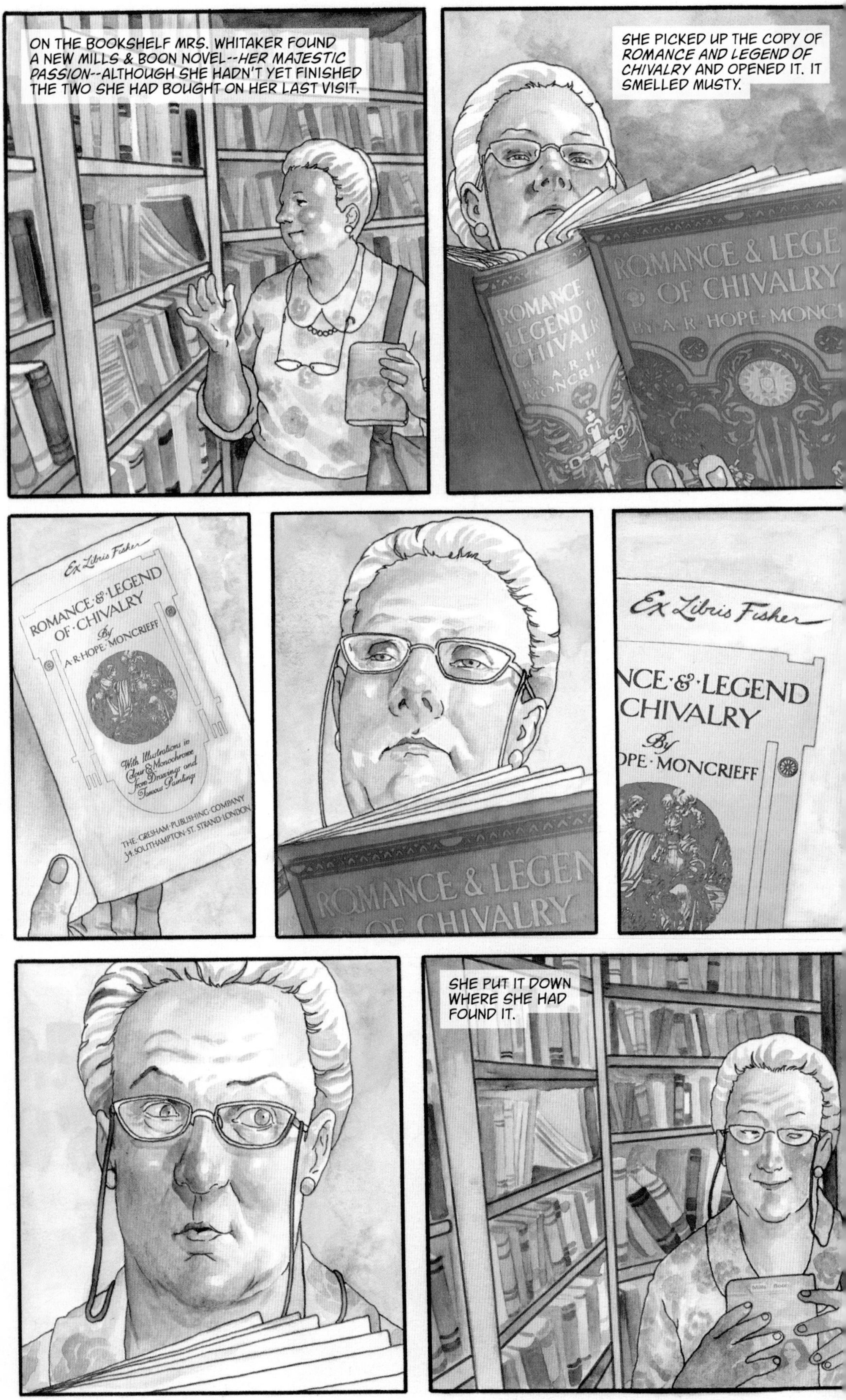
ON THE BOOKSHELF MRS. WHITAKER FOUND A NEW MILLS & BOON NOVEL--*HER MAJESTIC PASSION*--ALTHOUGH SHE HADN'T YET FINISHED THE TWO SHE HAD BOUGHT ON HER LAST VISIT.
SHE PICKED UP THE COPY OF *ROMANCE AND LEGEND OF CHIVALRY* AND OPENED IT. IT SMELLED MUSTY.
ROMANCE & LEGEND OF CHIVALRY
BY A. R. HOPE-MONCRIEFF
Ex Libris Fisher
ROMANCE & LEGEND OF CHIVALRY
By
A. R. HOPE MONCRIEFF
With Illustrations in Colour & Monochrome from Drawings and Famous Paintings
THE GRESHAM PUBLISHING COMPANY
34 SOUTHAMPTON ST. STRAND LONDON
ROMANCE & LEGEN
OF CHIVALRY
Ex Libris Fisher
NCE & LEGEND
CHIVALRY
By
OPE·MONCRIEFF
SHE PUT IT DOWN WHERE SHE HAD FOUND IT.

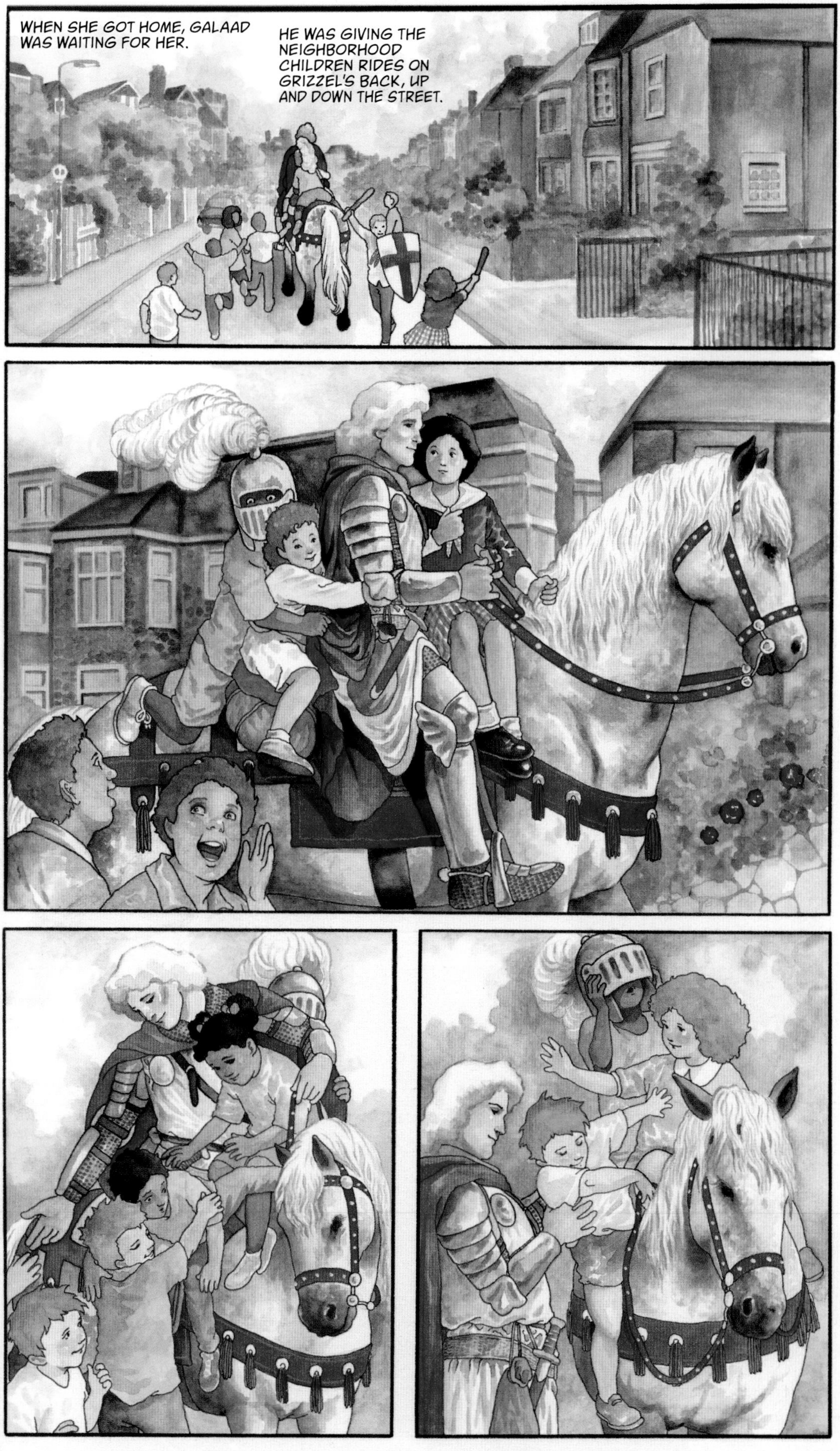
WHEN SHE GOT HOME, GALAAD WAS WAITING FOR HER.
HE WAS GIVING THE NEIGHBORHOOD CHILDREN RIDES ON GRIZZEL'S BACK, UP AND DOWN THE STREET.

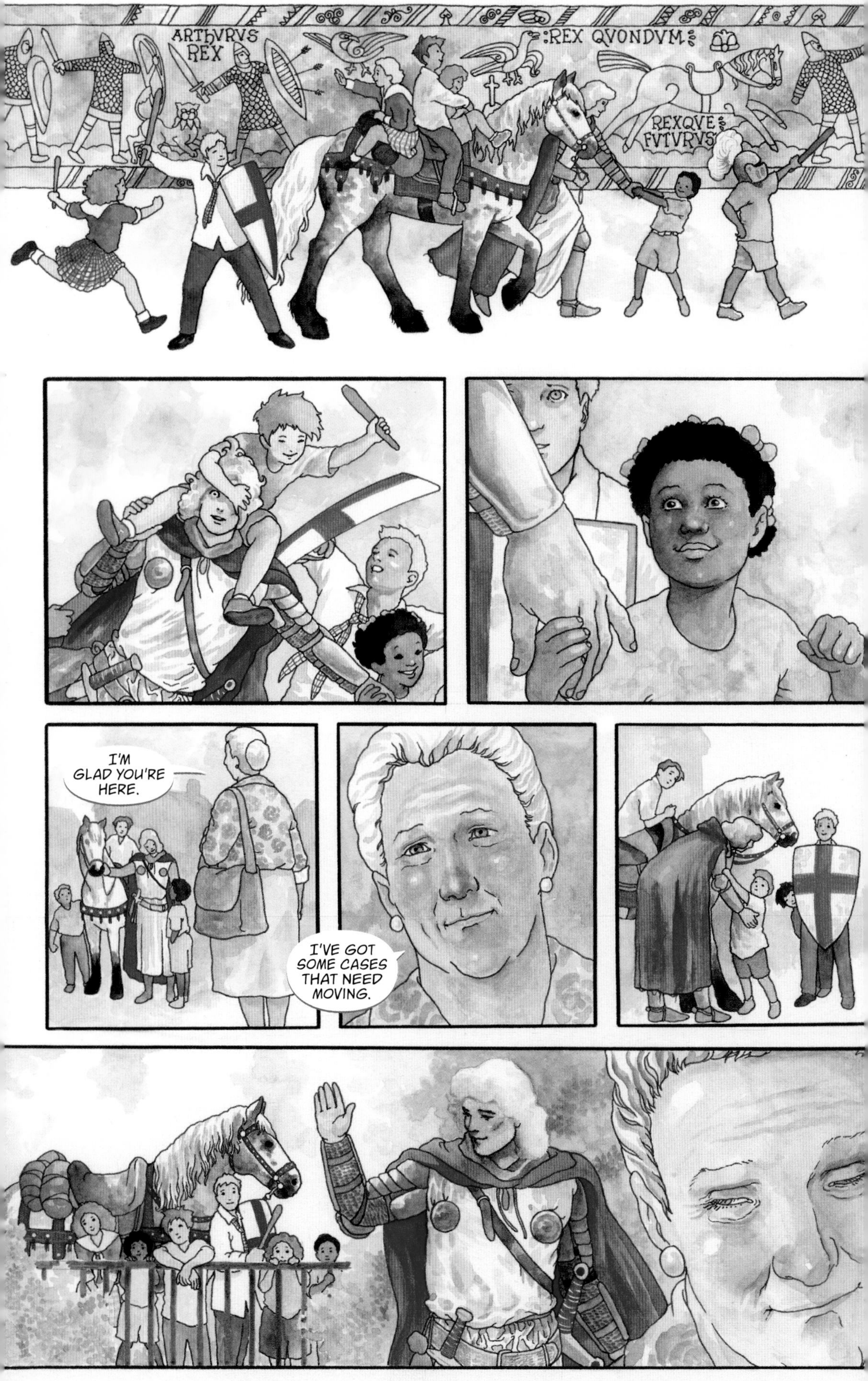
ARTHVRVS REX
:REX QVONDVM:
REXQVE FVTVRVS
I'M GLAD YOU'RE HERE.
I'VE GOT SOME CASES THAT NEED MOVING.

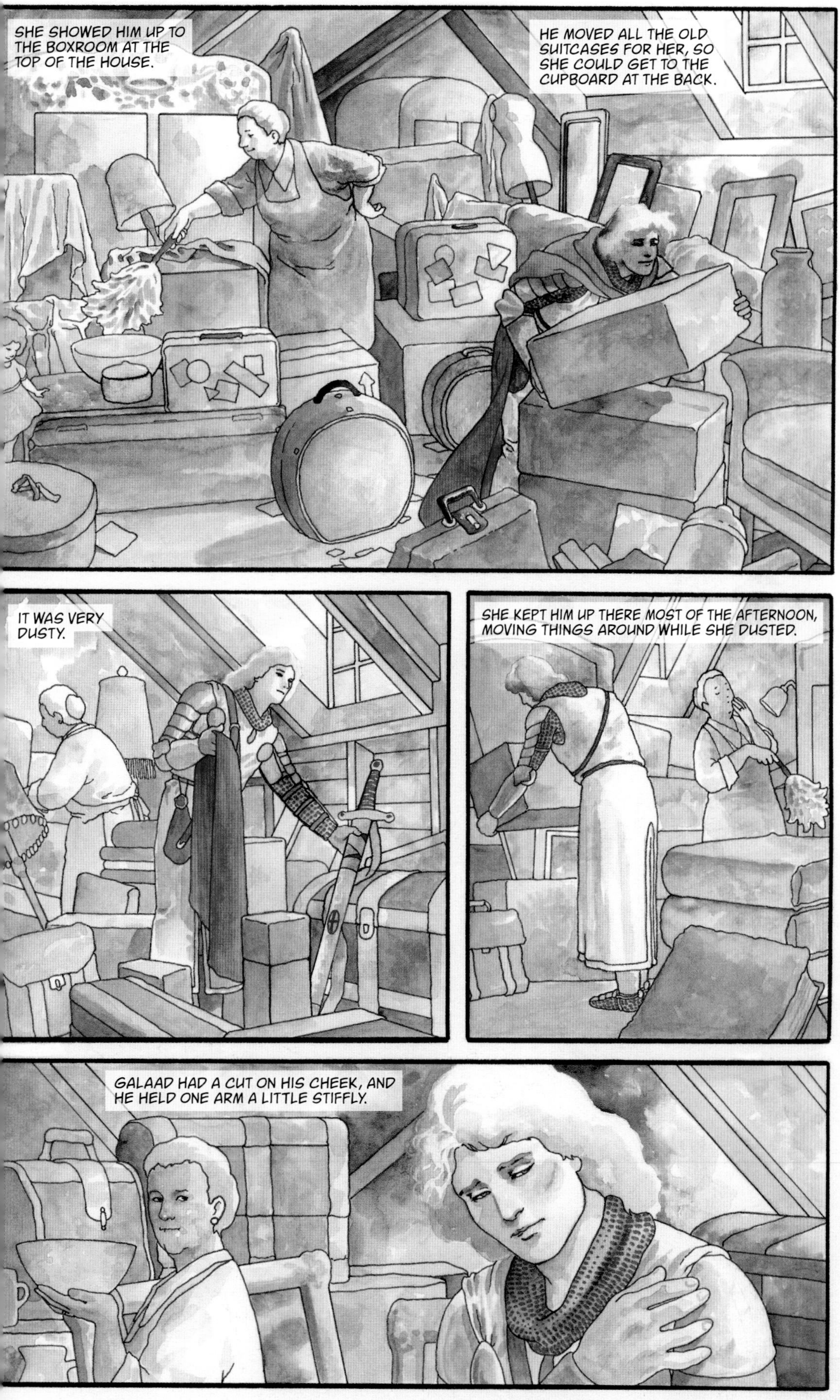
SHE SHOWED HIM UP TO THE BOXROOM AT THE TOP OF THE HOUSE.
HE MOVED ALL THE OLD SUITCASES FOR HER, SO SHE COULD GET TO THE CUPBOARD AT THE BACK.
IT WAS VERY DUSTY.
SHE KEPT HIM UP THERE MOST OF THE AFTERNOON, MOVING THINGS AROUND WHILE SHE DUSTED.
GALAAD HAD A CUT ON HIS CHEEK, AND HE HELD ONE ARM A LITTLE STIFFLY.

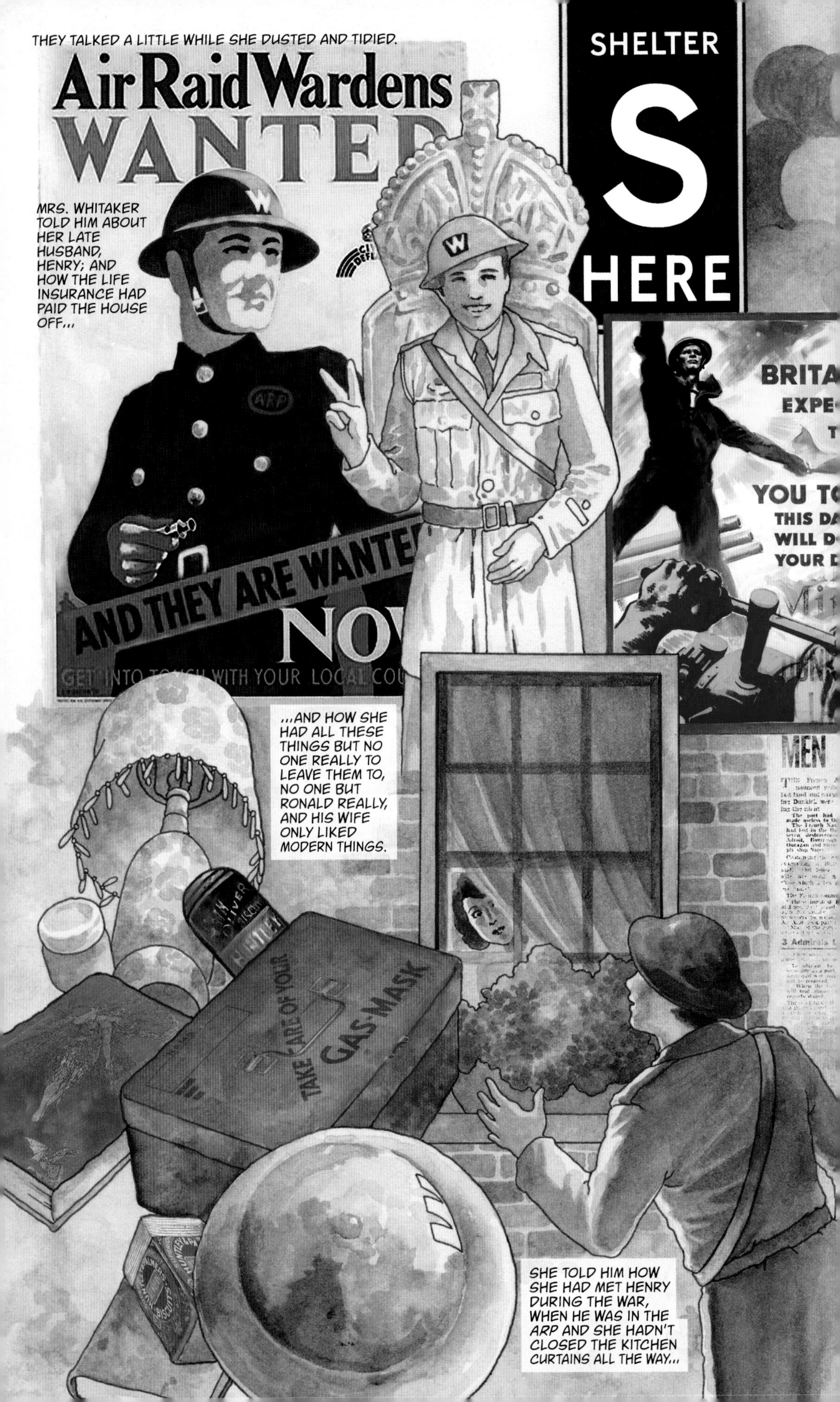
THEY TALKED A LITTLE WHILE SHE DUSTED AND TIDIED.
Air Raid Wardens
WANTE
MRS. WHITAKER TOLD HIM ABOUT HER LATE HUSBAND, HENRY; AND HOW THE LIFE INSURANCE HAD PAID THE HOUSE OFF...
W
W
ARP
AND THEY ARE WANTE
NOV
GET INTO TOUCH WITH YOUR LOCAL COU
SHELTER
S
HERE
BRITA
EXPE
YOU TO
THIS DA
WILL D
YOUR D
...AND HOW SHE HAD ALL THESE THINGS BUT NO ONE REALLY TO LEAVE THEM TO, NO ONE BUT RONALD REALLY, AND HIS WIFE ONLY LIKED MODERN THINGS.
MEN
3 Admirals
TAKE CARE OF YOUR GAS-MASK
SHE TOLD HIM HOW SHE HAD MET HENRY DURING THE WAR, WHEN HE WAS IN THE ARP AND SHE HADN'T CLOSED THE KITCHEN CURTAINS ALL THE WAY...

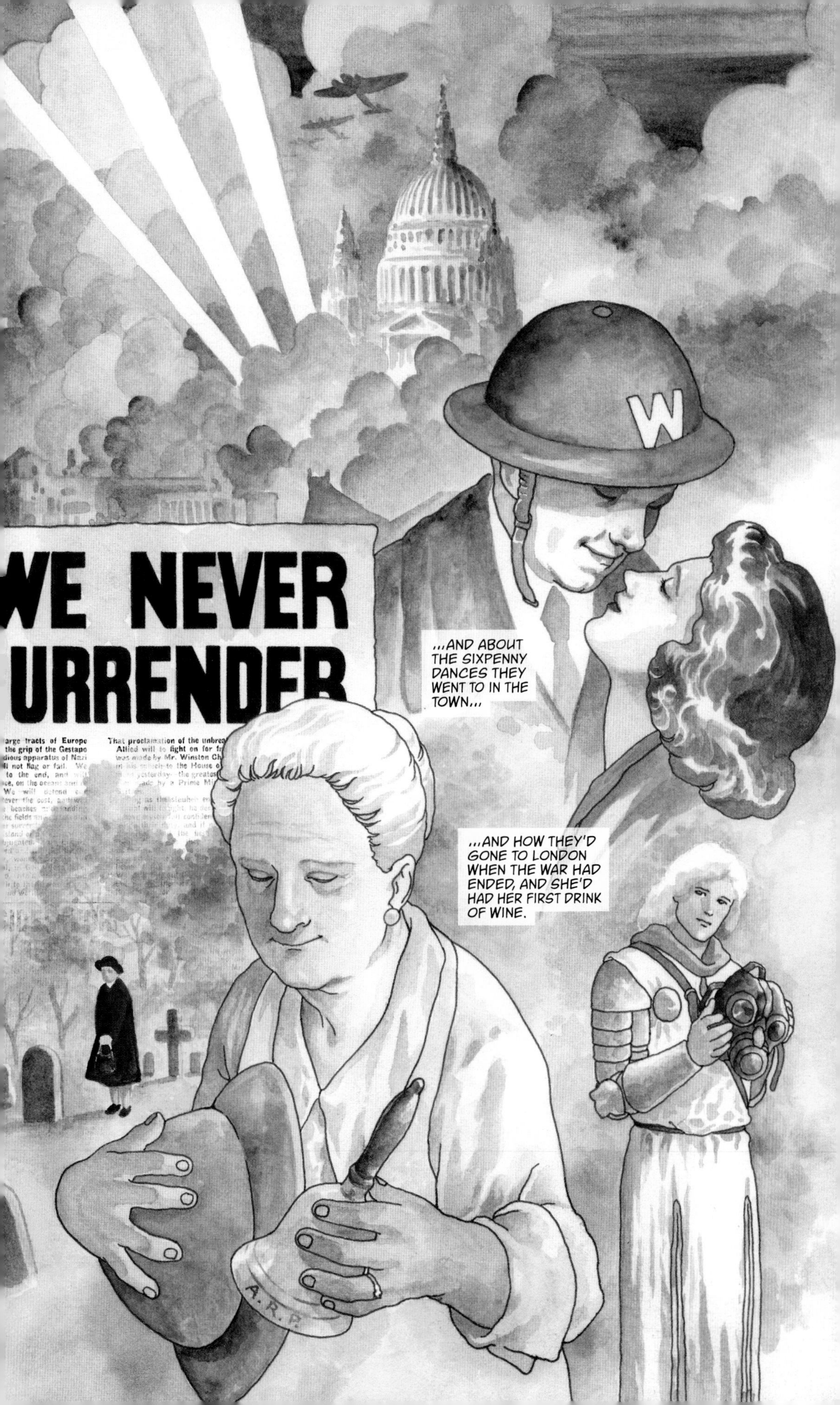
WE NEVER
URRENDER
...AND ABOUT THE SIXPENNY DANCES THEY WENT TO IN THE TOWN...
...AND HOW THEY'D GONE TO LONDON WHEN THE WAR HAD ENDED, AND SHE'D HAD HER FIRST DRINK OF WINE.
A.R.P.

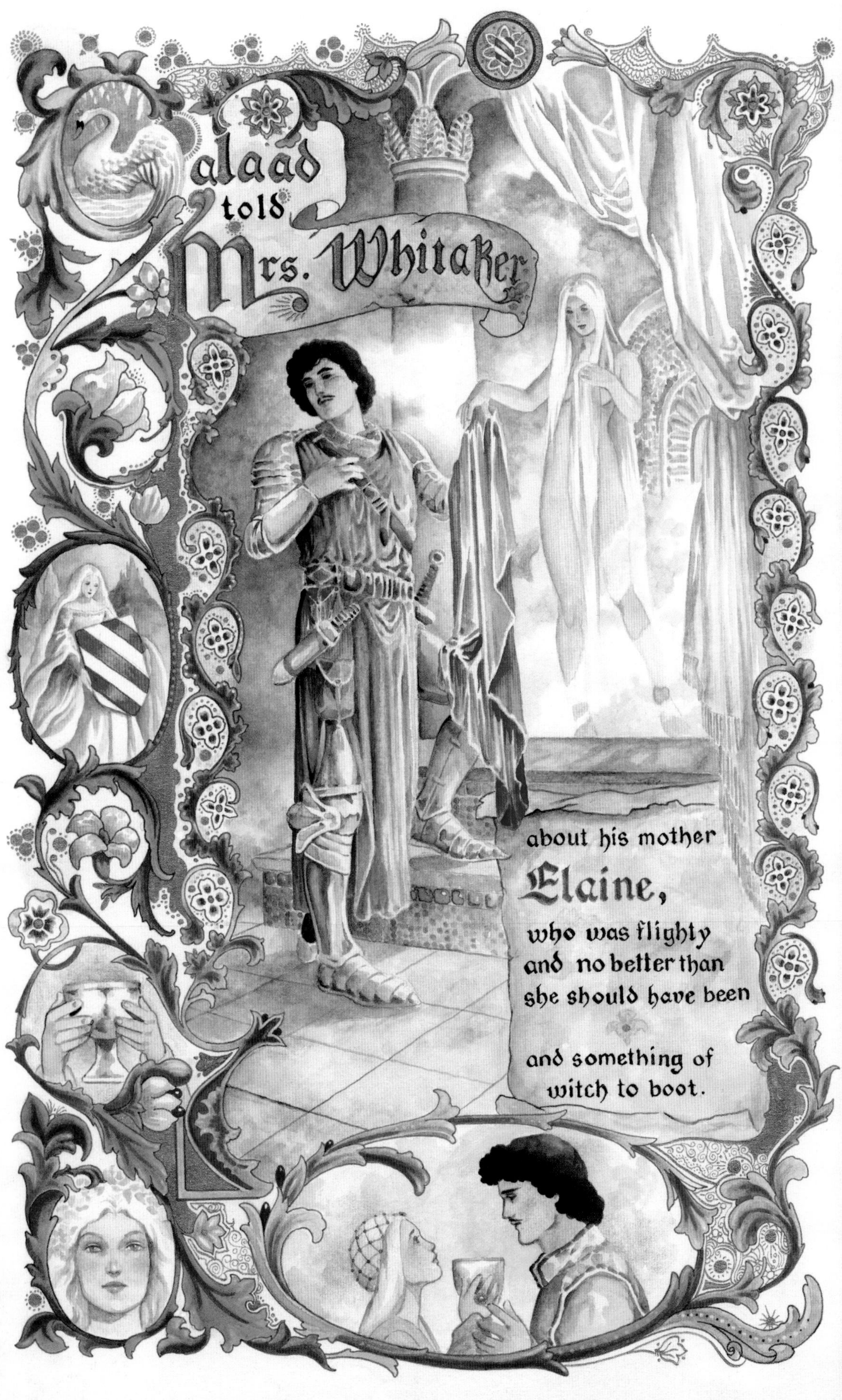
Galaad
told
Mrs. Whitaker
about his mother
Elaine,
who was flighty
and no better than
she should have been
and something of
witch to boot.

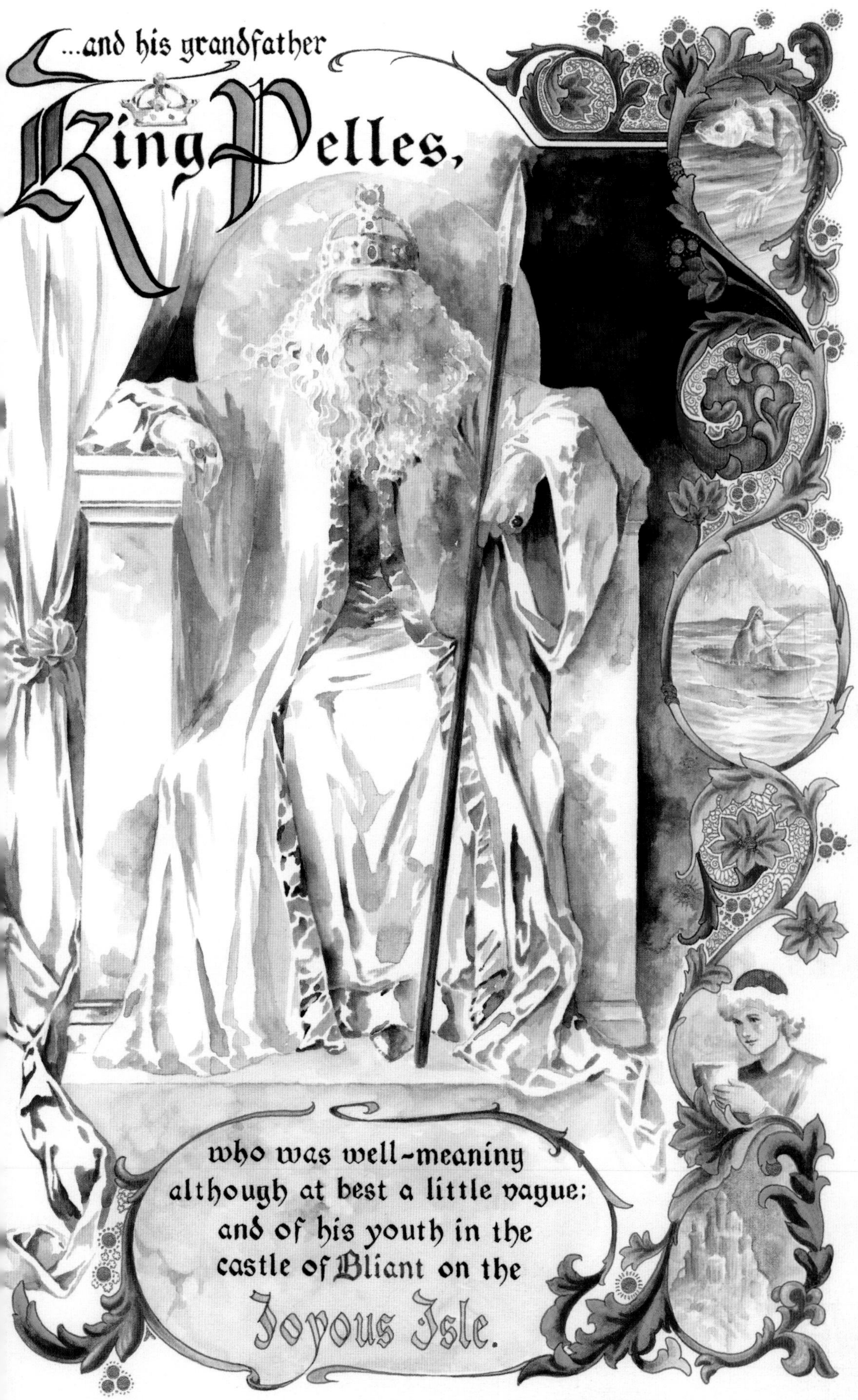
...and his grandfather
King Pelles,
who was well-meaning
although at best a little vague;
and of his youth in the
castle of Bliant on the
Joyous Isle.

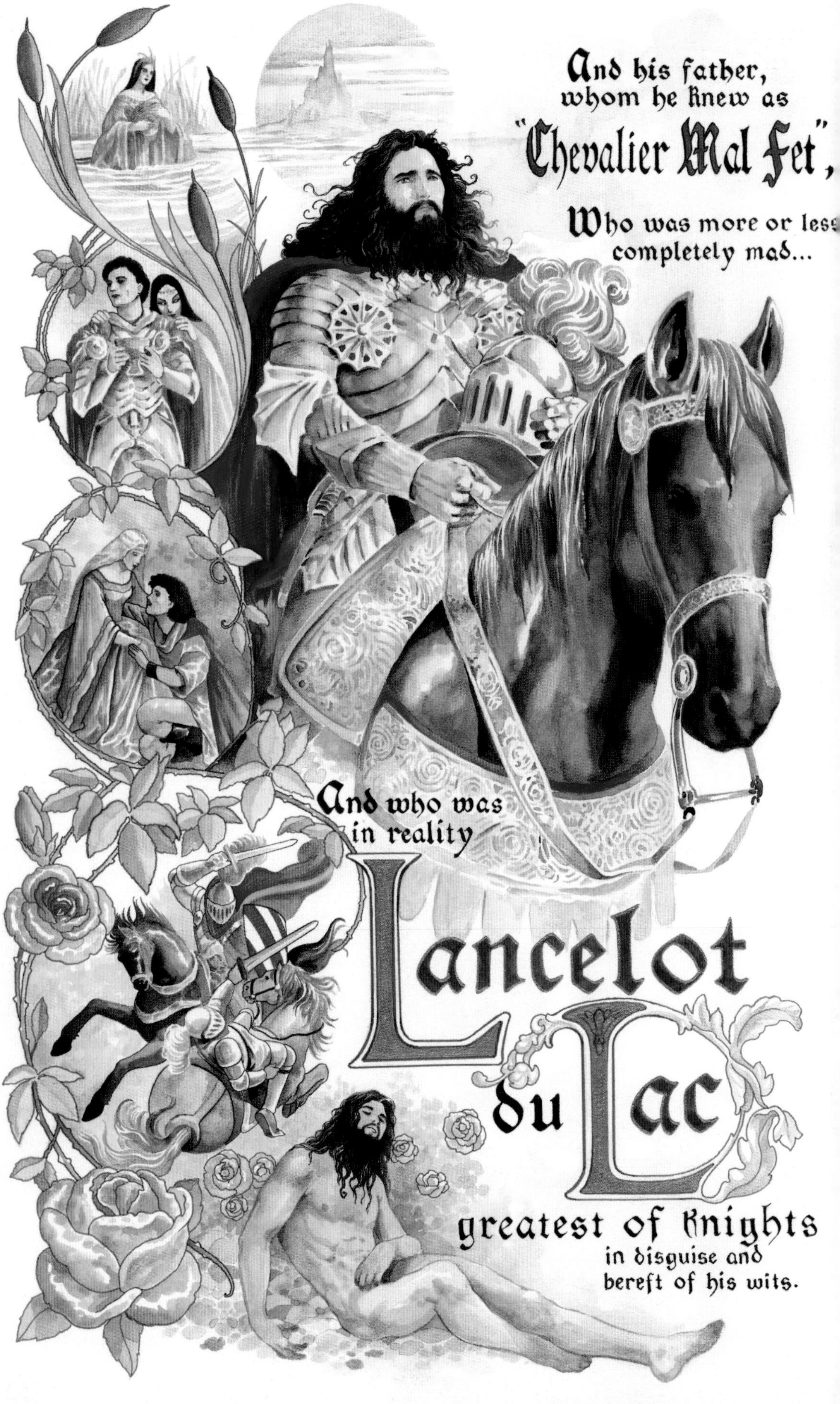
And his father,
whom he knew as
"Chevalier Mal Fet",
Who was more or les
completely mad...
And who was
in reality
Lancelot
du Lac
greatest of knights
in disguise and
bereft of his wits.

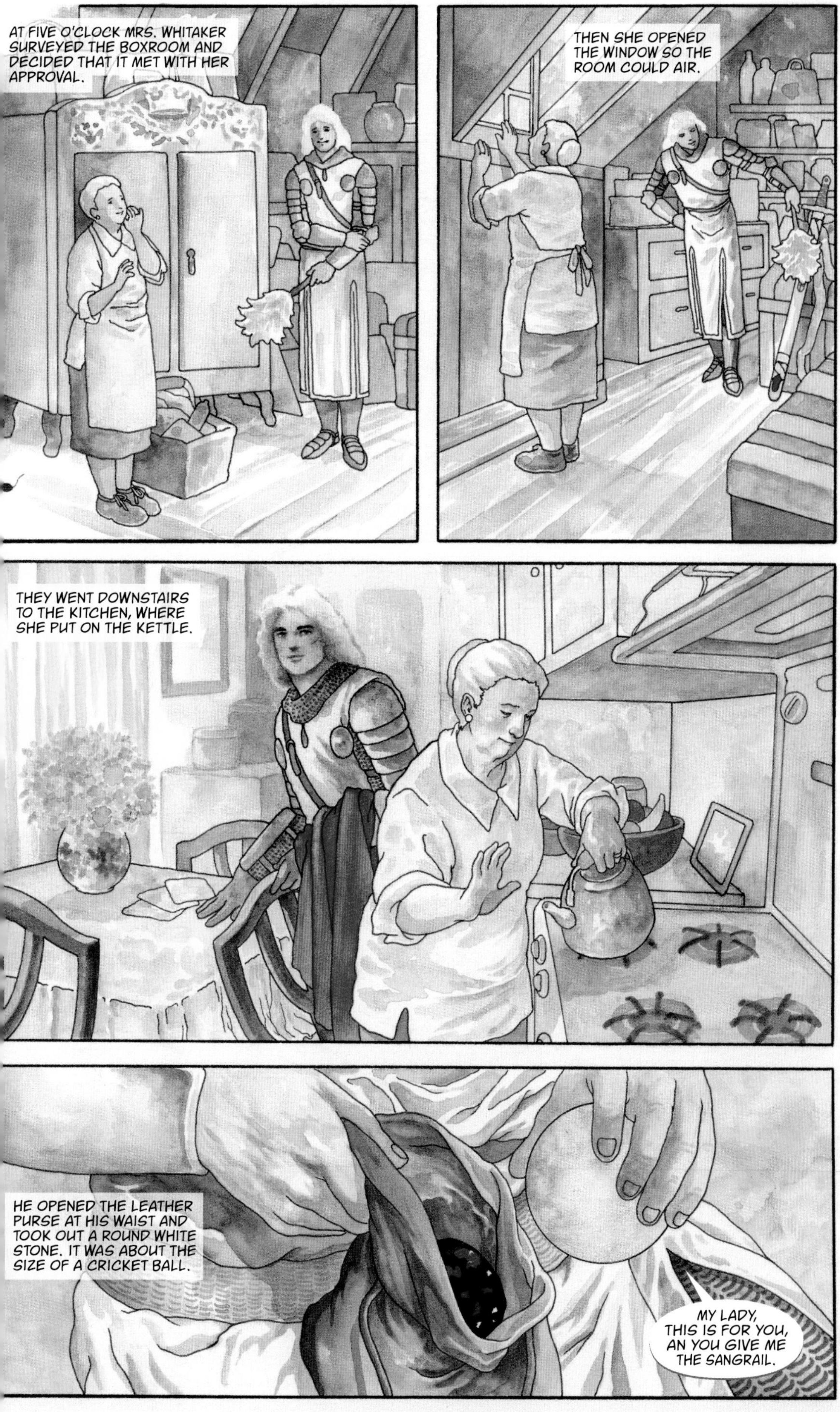
AT FIVE O'CLOCK MRS. WHITAKER SURVEYED THE BOXROOM AND DECIDED THAT IT MET WITH HER APPROVAL.
THEN SHE OPENED THE WINDOW SO THE ROOM COULD AIR.
THEY WENT DOWNSTAIRS TO THE KITCHEN, WHERE SHE PUT ON THE KETTLE.
HE OPENED THE LEATHER PURSE AT HIS WAIST AND TOOK OUT A ROUND WHITE STONE. IT WAS ABOUT THE SIZE OF A CRICKET BALL.
MY LADY, THIS IS FOR YOU, AN YOU GIVE ME THE SANGRAIL.

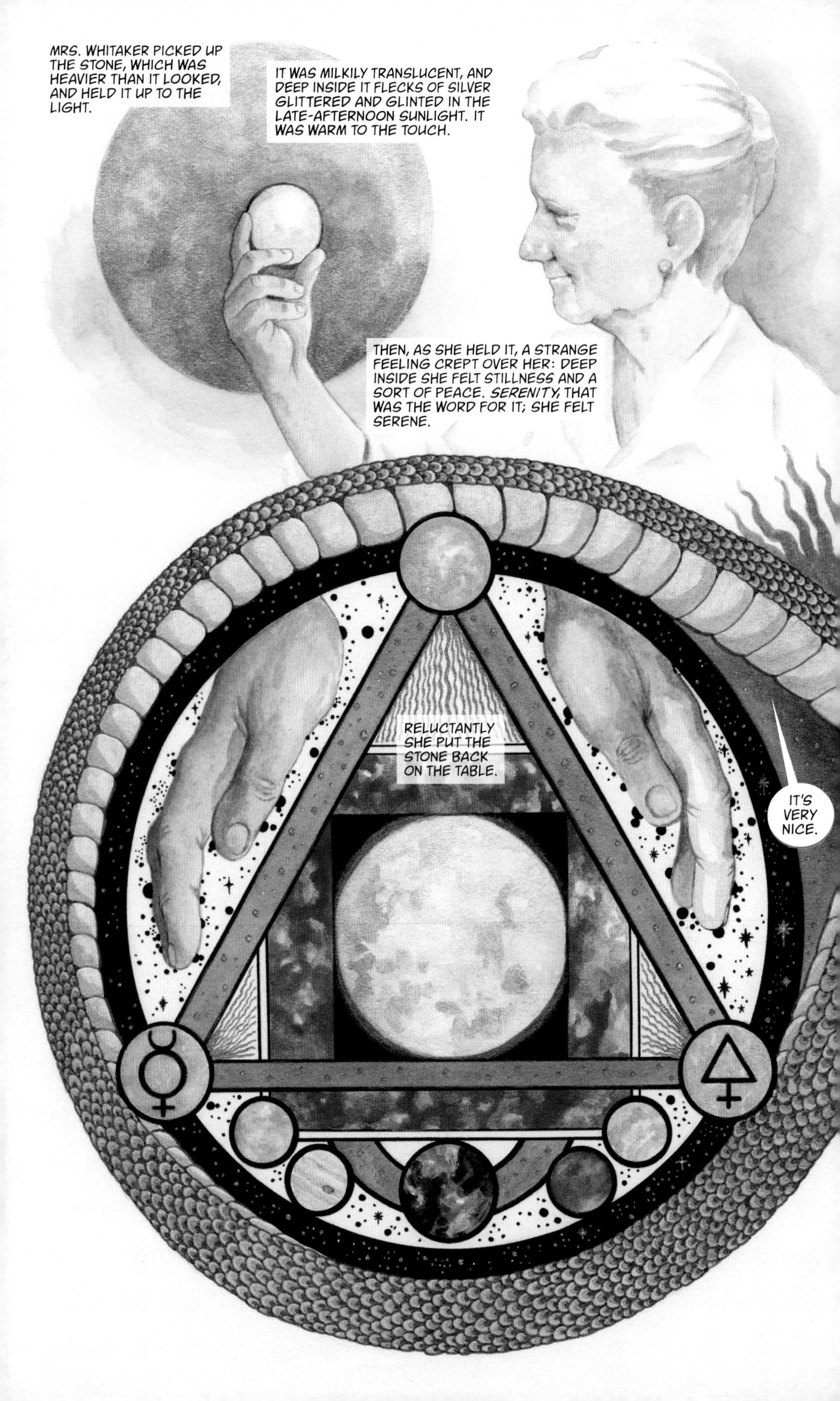
MRS. WHITAKER PICKED UP THE STONE, WHICH WAS HEAVIER THAN IT LOOKED, AND HELD IT UP TO THE LIGHT.
IT WAS MILKILY TRANSLUCENT, AND DEEP INSIDE IT FLECKS OF SILVER GLITTERED AND GLINTED IN THE LATE-AFTERNOON SUNLIGHT. IT WAS WARM TO THE TOUCH.
THEN, AS SHE HELD IT, A STRANGE FEELING CREPT OVER HER: DEEP INSIDE SHE FELT STILLNESS AND A SORT OF PEACE. *SERENITY*, THAT WAS THE WORD FOR IT; SHE FELT SERENE.
RELUCTANTLY SHE PUT THE STONE BACK ON THE TABLE.
IT'S VERY NICE.

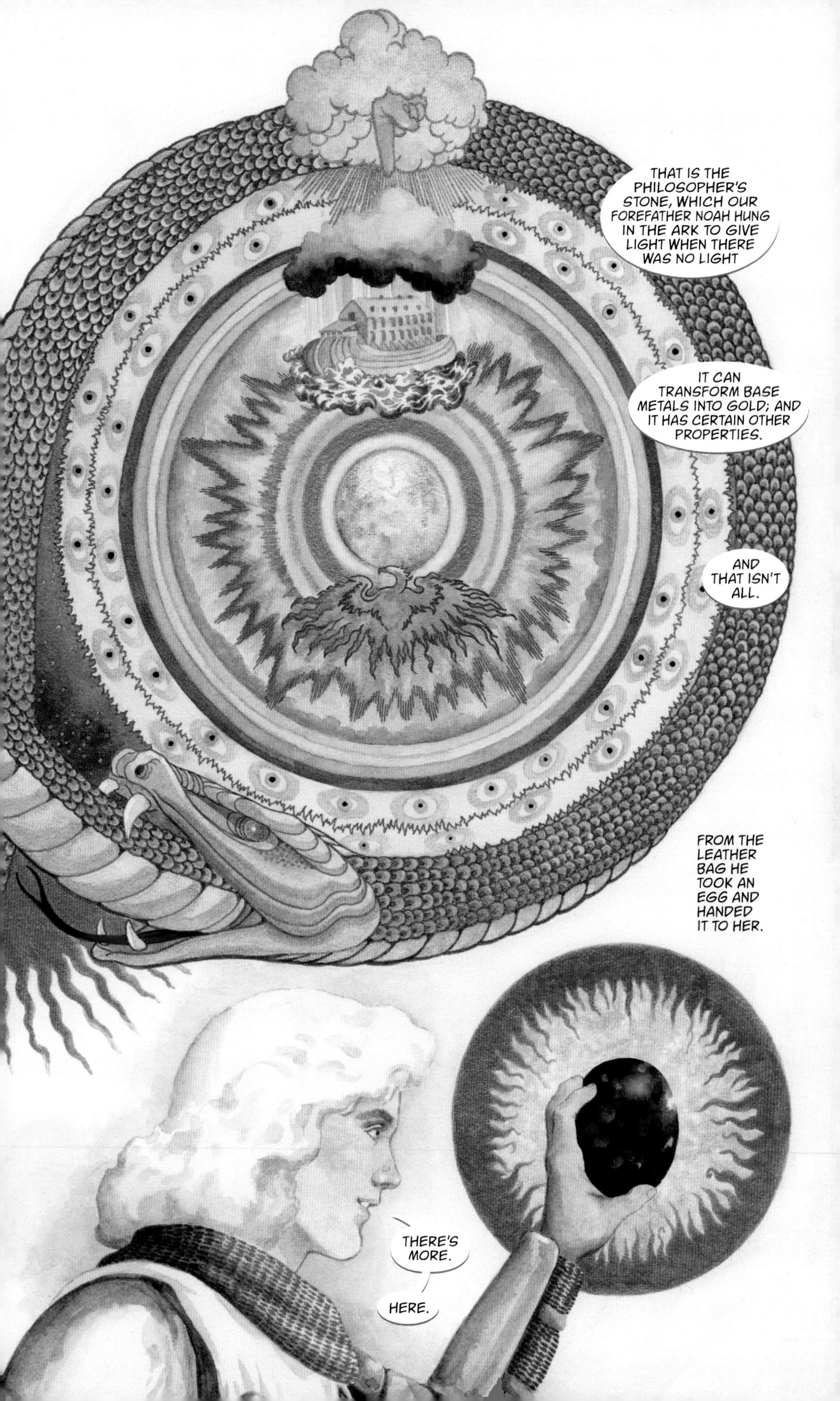
THAT IS THE PHILOSOPHER'S STONE, WHICH OUR FOREFATHER NOAH HUNG IN THE ARK TO GIVE LIGHT WHEN THERE WAS NO LIGHT
IT CAN TRANSFORM BASE METALS INTO GOLD; AND IT HAS CERTAIN OTHER PROPERTIES.
AND THAT ISN'T ALL.
FROM THE LEATHER BAG HE TOOK AN EGG AND HANDED IT TO HER.
THERE'S MORE.
HERE.

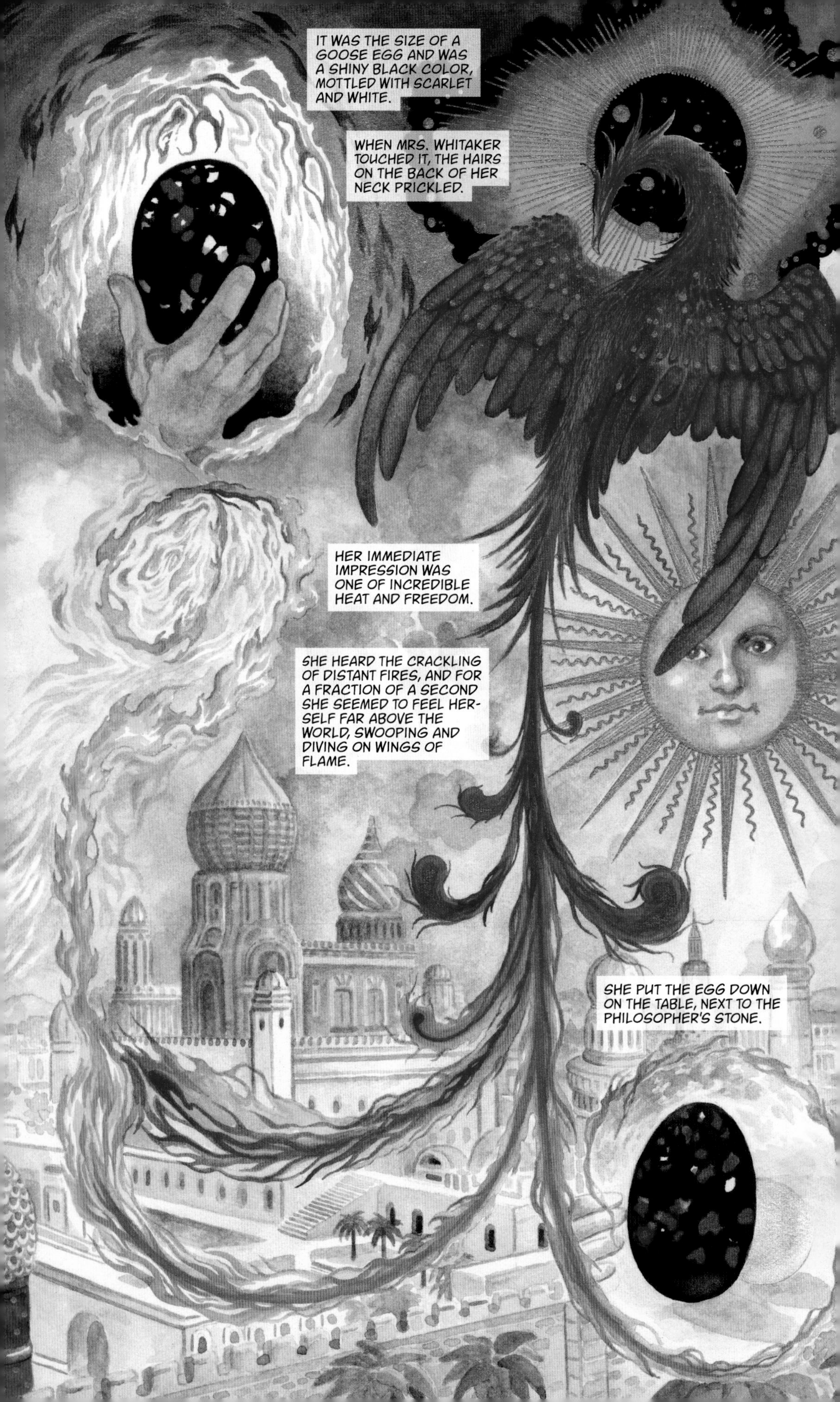
IT WAS THE SIZE OF A GOOSE EGG AND WAS A SHINY BLACK COLOR, MOTTLED WITH SCARLET AND WHITE.
WHEN MRS. WHITAKER TOUCHED IT, THE HAIRS ON THE BACK OF HER NECK PRICKLED.
HER IMMEDIATE IMPRESSION WAS ONE OF INCREDIBLE HEAT AND FREEDOM.
SHE HEARD THE CRACKLING OF DISTANT FIRES, AND FOR A FRACTION OF A SECOND SHE SEEMED TO FEEL HER-SELF FAR ABOVE THE WORLD, SWOOPING AND DIVING ON WINGS OF FLAME.
SHE PUT THE EGG DOWN ON THE TABLE, NEXT TO THE PHILOSOPHER'S STONE.

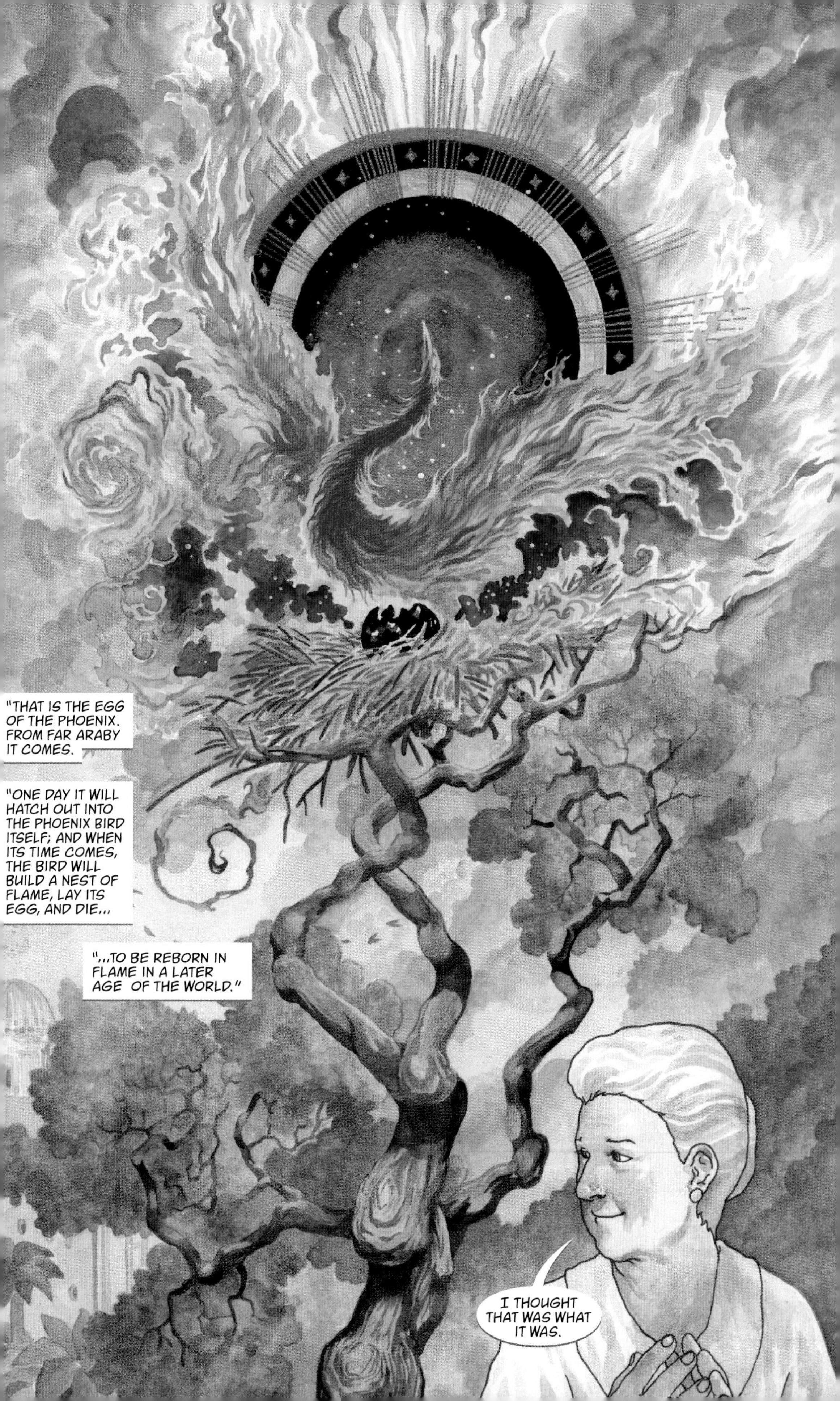
"THAT IS THE EGG OF THE PHOENIX. FROM FAR ARABY IT COMES.
"ONE DAY IT WILL HATCH OUT INTO THE PHOENIX BIRD ITSELF; AND WHEN ITS TIME COMES, THE BIRD WILL BUILD A NEST OF FLAME, LAY ITS EGG, AND DIE...
"...TO BE REBORN IN FLAME IN A LATER AGE OF THE WORLD."
I THOUGHT THAT WAS WHAT IT WAS.

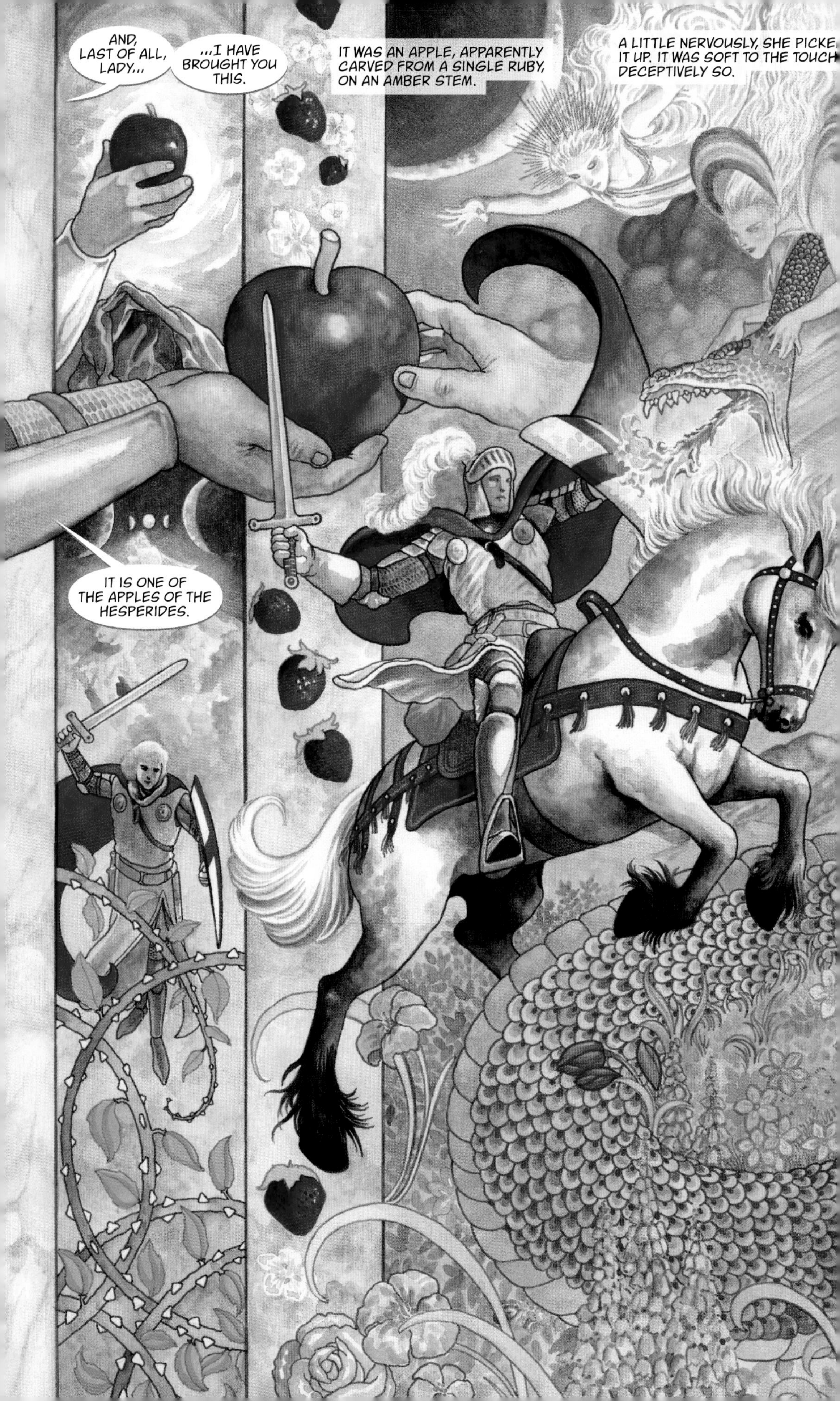

AND, LAST OF ALL, LADY...
...I HAVE BROUGHT YOU THIS.
IT WAS AN APPLE, APPARENTLY CARVED FROM A SINGLE RUBY, ON AN AMBER STEM.
A LITTLE NERVOUSLY, SHE PICKE IT UP. IT WAS SOFT TO THE TOUCH DECEPTIVELY SO.
IT IS ONE OF THE APPLES OF THE HESPERIDES.

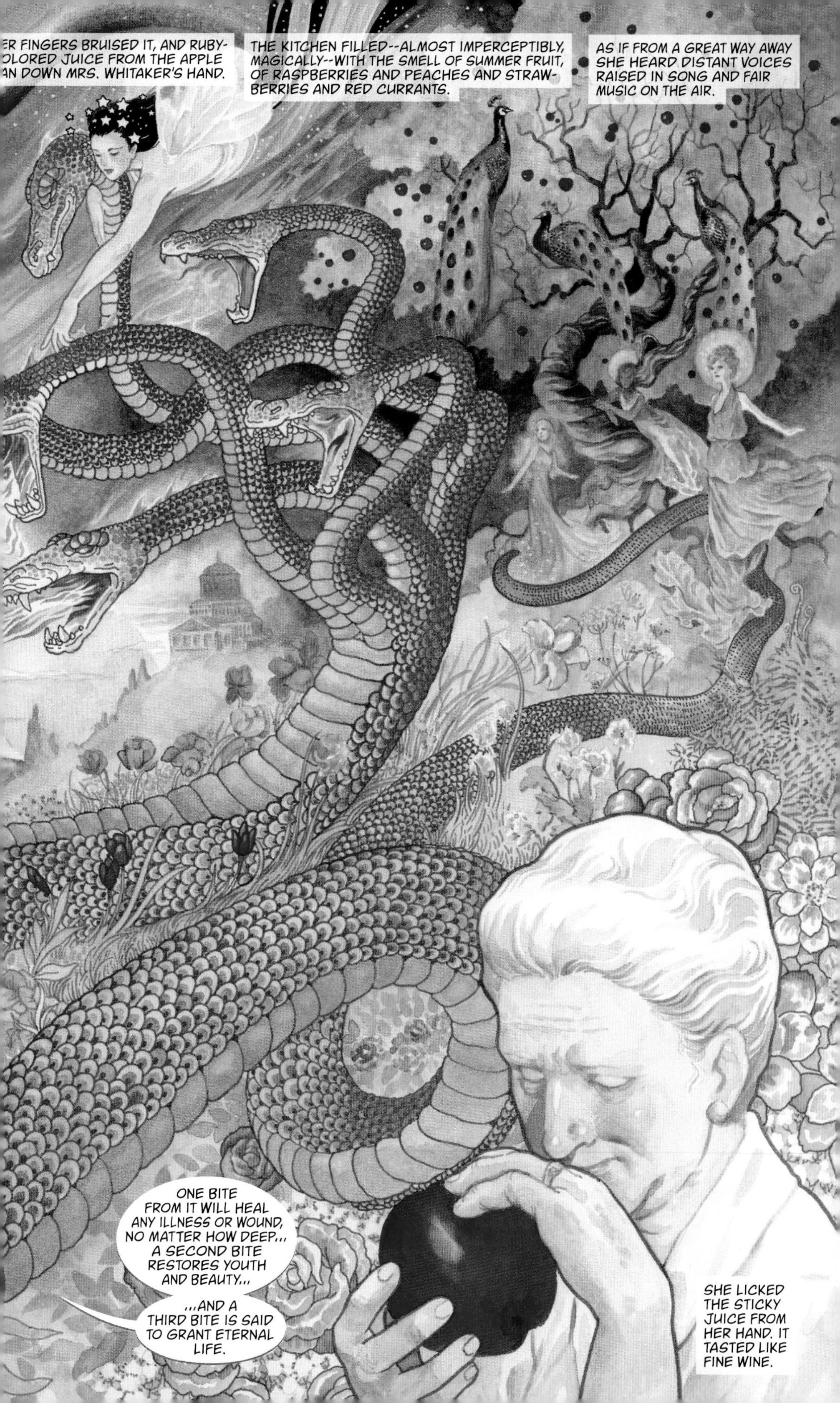
ER FINGERS BRUISED IT, AND RUBY-
OLORED JUICE FROM THE APPLE
AN DOWN MRS. WHITAKER'S HAND.
THE KITCHEN FILLED--ALMOST IMPERCEPTIBLY, MAGICALLY--WITH THE SMELL OF SUMMER FRUIT, OF RASPBERRIES AND PEACHES AND STRAWBERRIES AND RED CURRANTS.
AS IF FROM A GREAT WAY AWAY SHE HEARD DISTANT VOICES RAISED IN SONG AND FAIR MUSIC ON THE AIR.
ONE BITE FROM IT WILL HEAL ANY ILLNESS OR WOUND, NO MATTER HOW DEEP... A SECOND BITE RESTORES YOUTH AND BEAUTY...
...AND A THIRD BITE IS SAID TO GRANT ETERNAL LIFE.
SHE LICKED THE STICKY JUICE FROM HER HAND. IT TASTED LIKE FINE WINE.

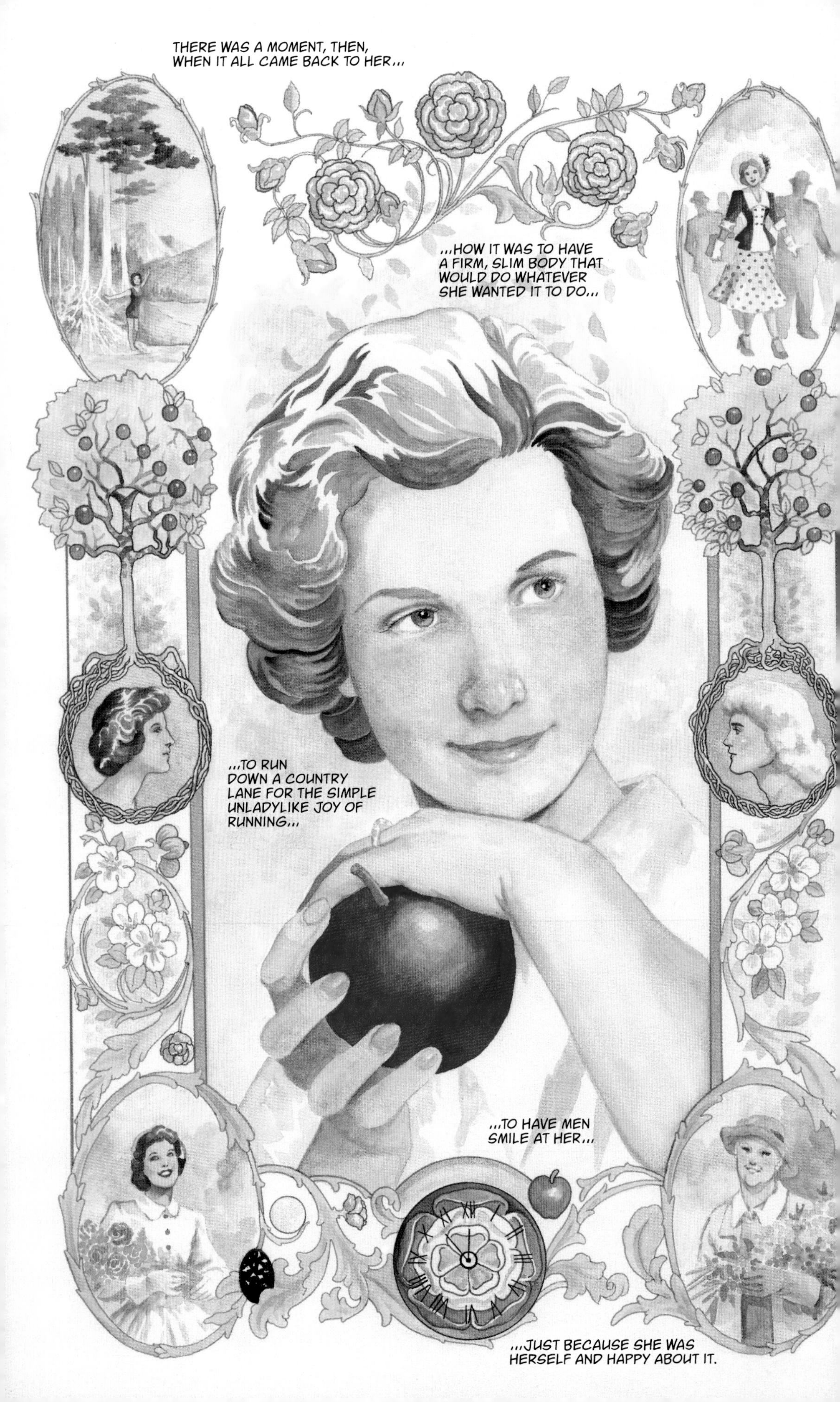
THERE WAS A MOMENT, THEN, WHEN IT ALL CAME BACK TO HER...
...HOW IT WAS TO HAVE A FIRM, SLIM BODY THAT WOULD DO WHATEVER SHE WANTED IT TO DO...
...TO RUN DOWN A COUNTRY LANE FOR THE SIMPLE UNLADYLIKE JOY OF RUNNING...
...TO HAVE MEN SMILE AT HER...
...JUST BECAUSE SHE WAS HERSELF AND HAPPY ABOUT IT.

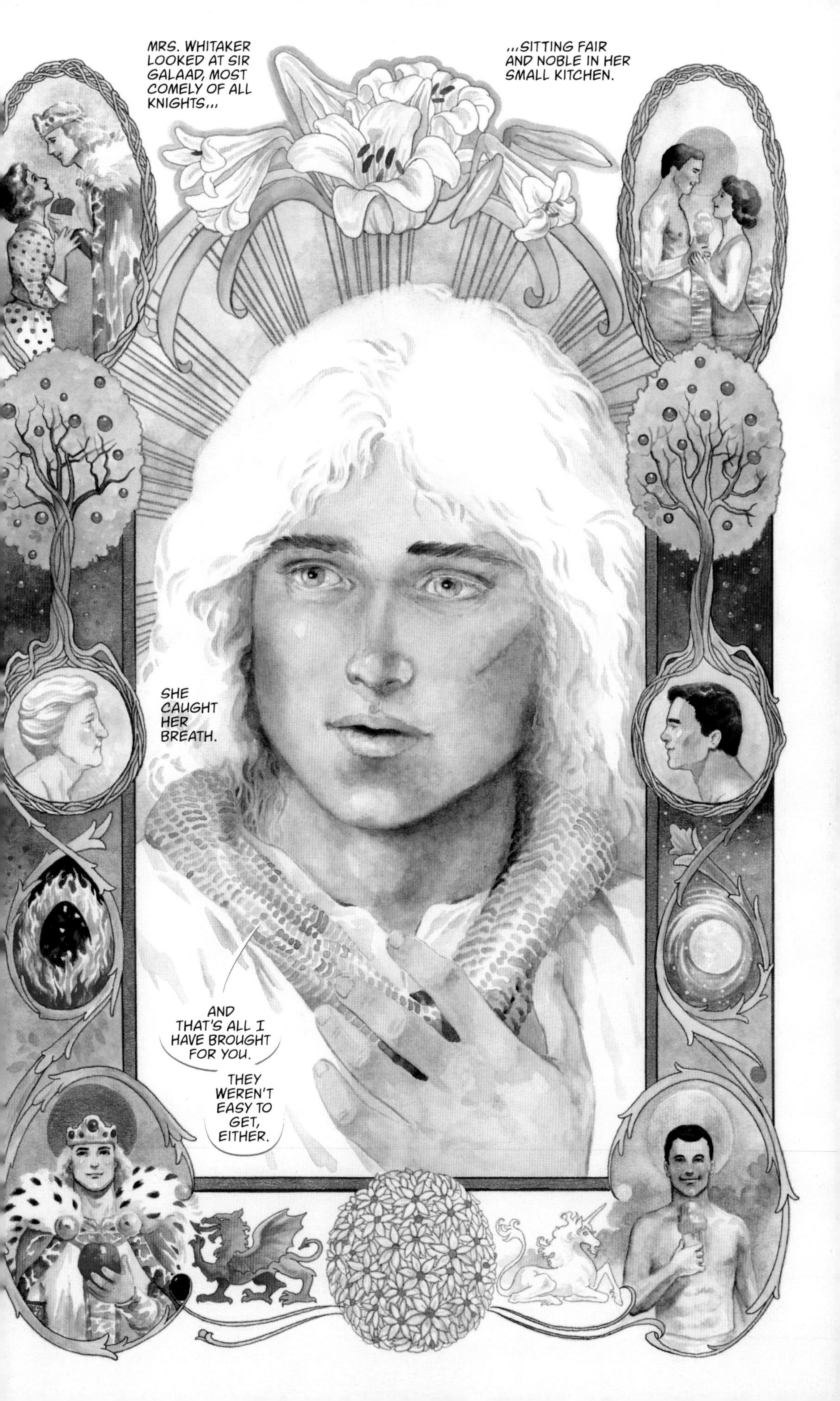
MRS. WHITAKER LOOKED AT SIR GALAAD, MOST COMELY OF ALL KNIGHTS...
...SITTING FAIR AND NOBLE IN HER SMALL KITCHEN.
SHE CAUGHT HER BREATH.
AND THAT'S ALL I HAVE BROUGHT FOR YOU.
THEY WEREN'T EASY TO GET, EITHER.

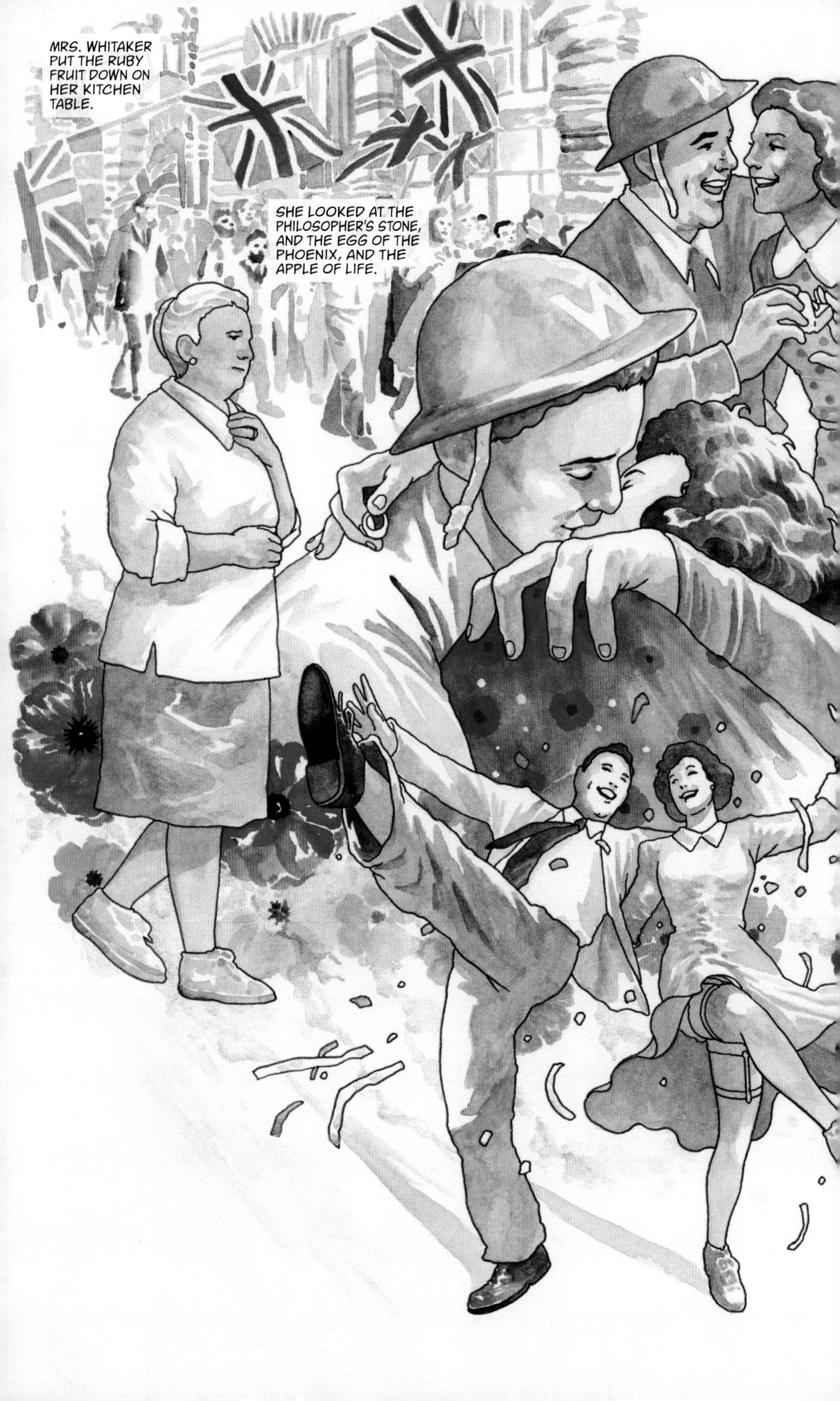
MRS. WHITAKER PUT THE RUBY FRUIT DOWN ON HER KITCHEN TABLE.
SHE LOOKED AT THE PHILOSOPHER'S STONE, AND THE EGG OF THE PHOENIX, AND THE APPLE OF LIFE.

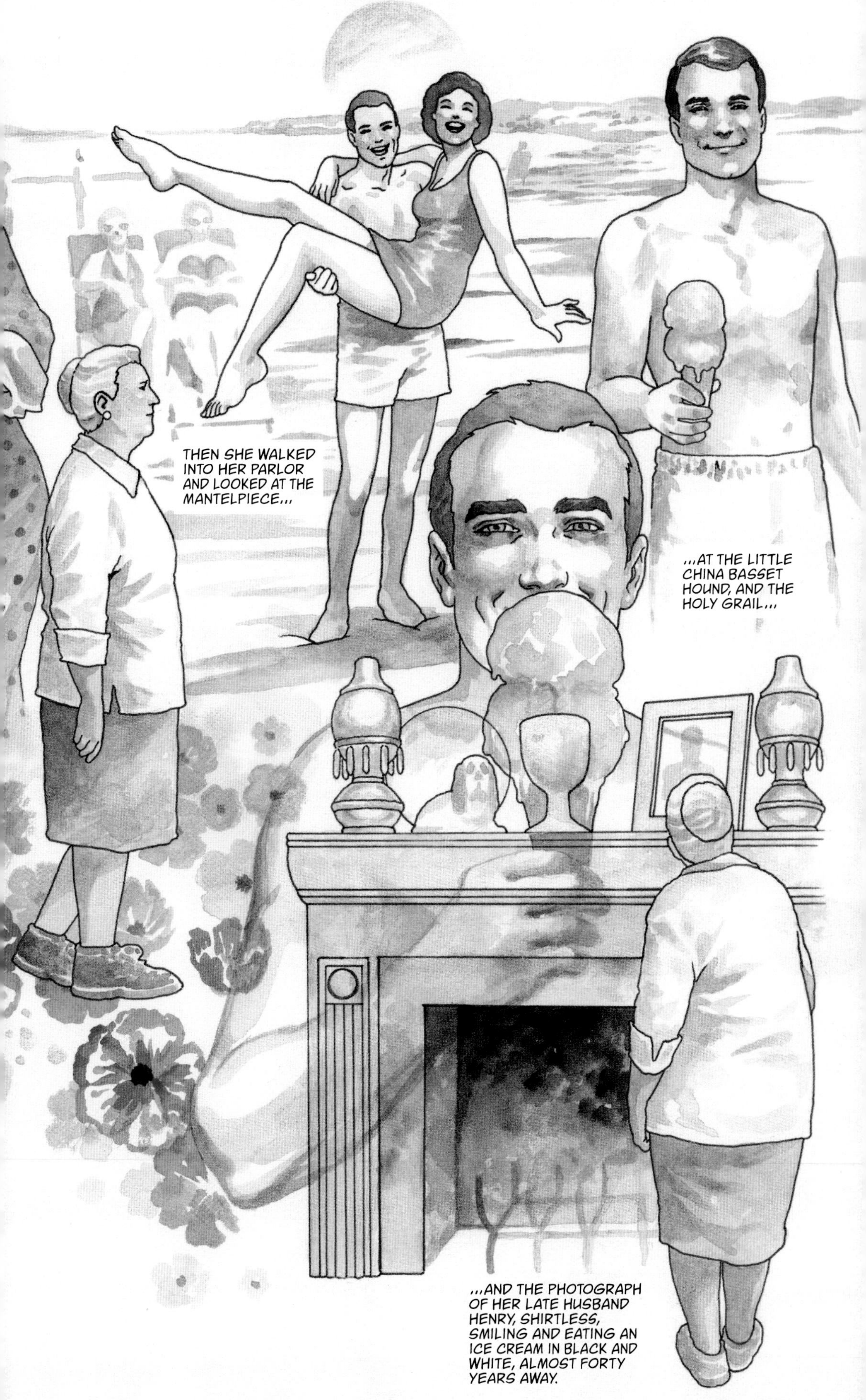
THEN SHE WALKED INTO HER PARLOR AND LOOKED AT THE MANTELPIECE...
...AT THE LITTLE CHINA BASSET HOUND, AND THE HOLY GRAIL...
...AND THE PHOTOGRAPH OF HER LATE HUSBAND HENRY, SHIRTLESS, SMILING AND EATING AN ICE CREAM IN BLACK AND WHITE, ALMOST FORTY YEARS AWAY.

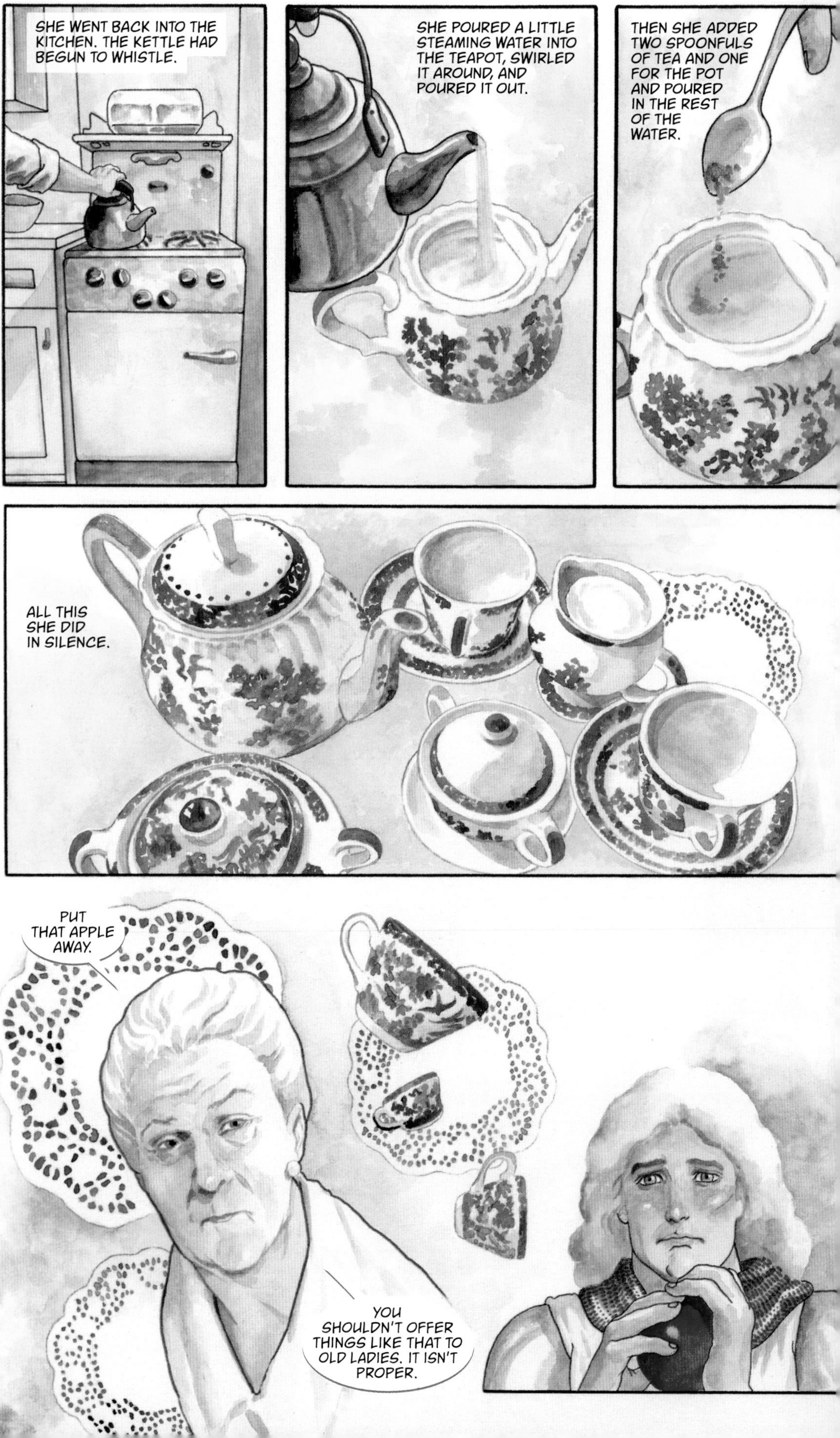
SHE WENT BACK INTO THE KITCHEN. THE KETTLE HAD BEGUN TO WHISTLE.
SHE POURED A LITTLE STEAMING WATER INTO THE TEAPOT, SWIRLED IT AROUND, AND POURED IT OUT.
THEN SHE ADDED TWO SPOONFULS OF TEA AND ONE FOR THE POT AND POURED IN THE REST OF THE WATER.
ALL THIS SHE DID IN SILENCE.
PUT THAT APPLE AWAY.
YOU SHOULDN'T OFFER THINGS LIKE THAT TO OLD LADIES. IT ISN'T PROPER.

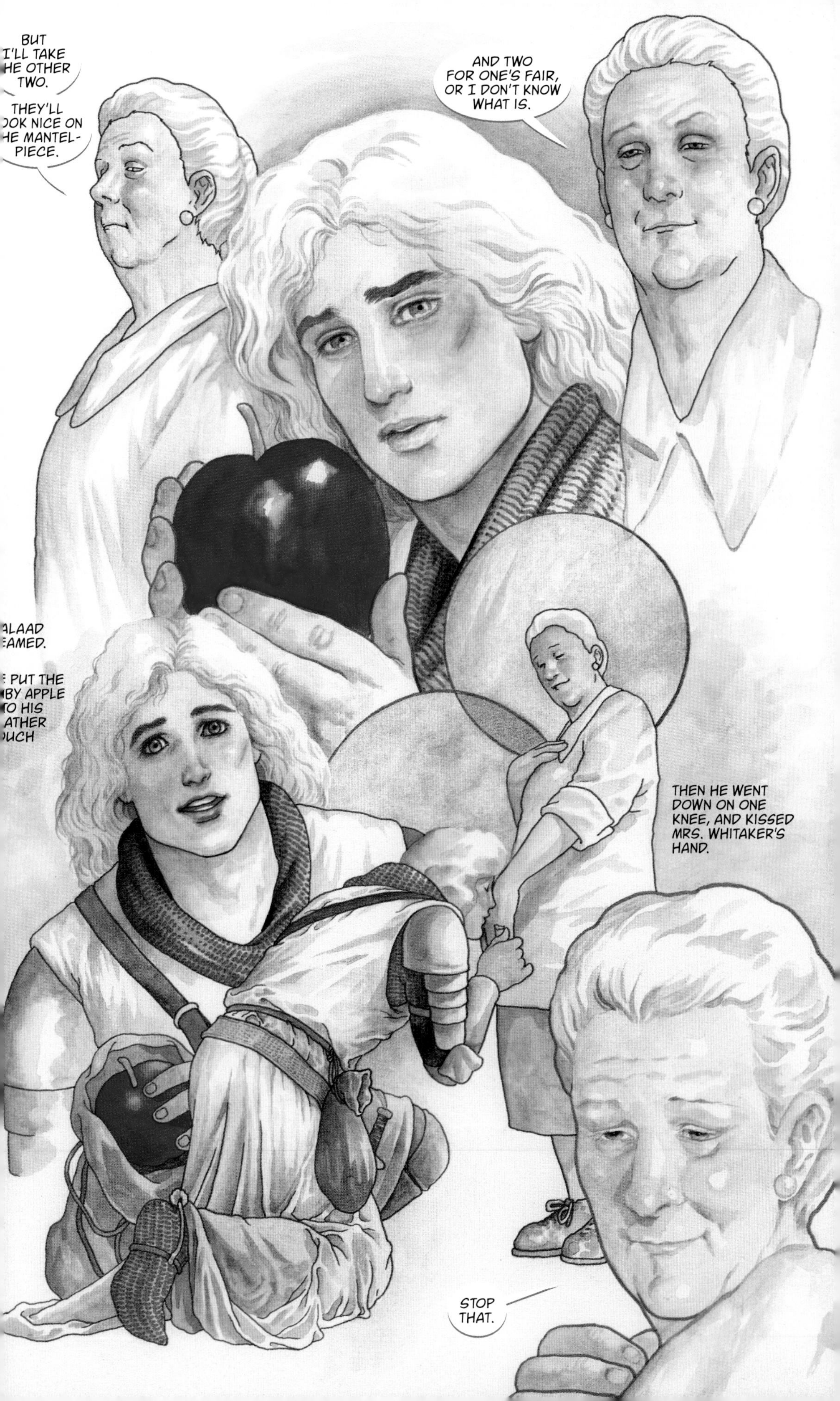
BUT I'LL TAKE HE OTHER TWO.
THEY'LL OOK NICE ON HE MANTEL-PIECE.
AND TWO FOR ONE'S FAIR, OR I DON'T KNOW WHAT IS.
ALAAD EAMED.
E PUT THE BY APPLE TO HIS ATHER UCH
THEN HE WENT DOWN ON ONE KNEE, AND KISSED MRS. WHITAKER'S HAND.
STOP THAT.

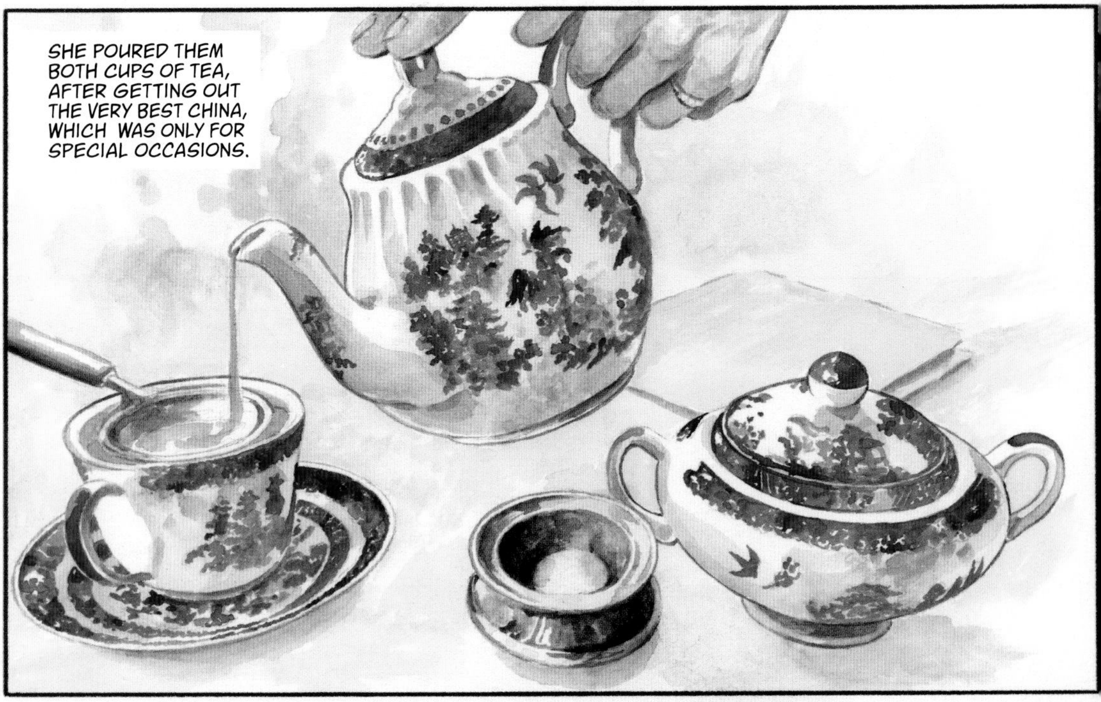
SHE POURED THEM BOTH CUPS OF TEA, AFTER GETTING OUT THE VERY BEST CHINA, WHICH WAS ONLY FOR SPECIAL OCCASIONS.

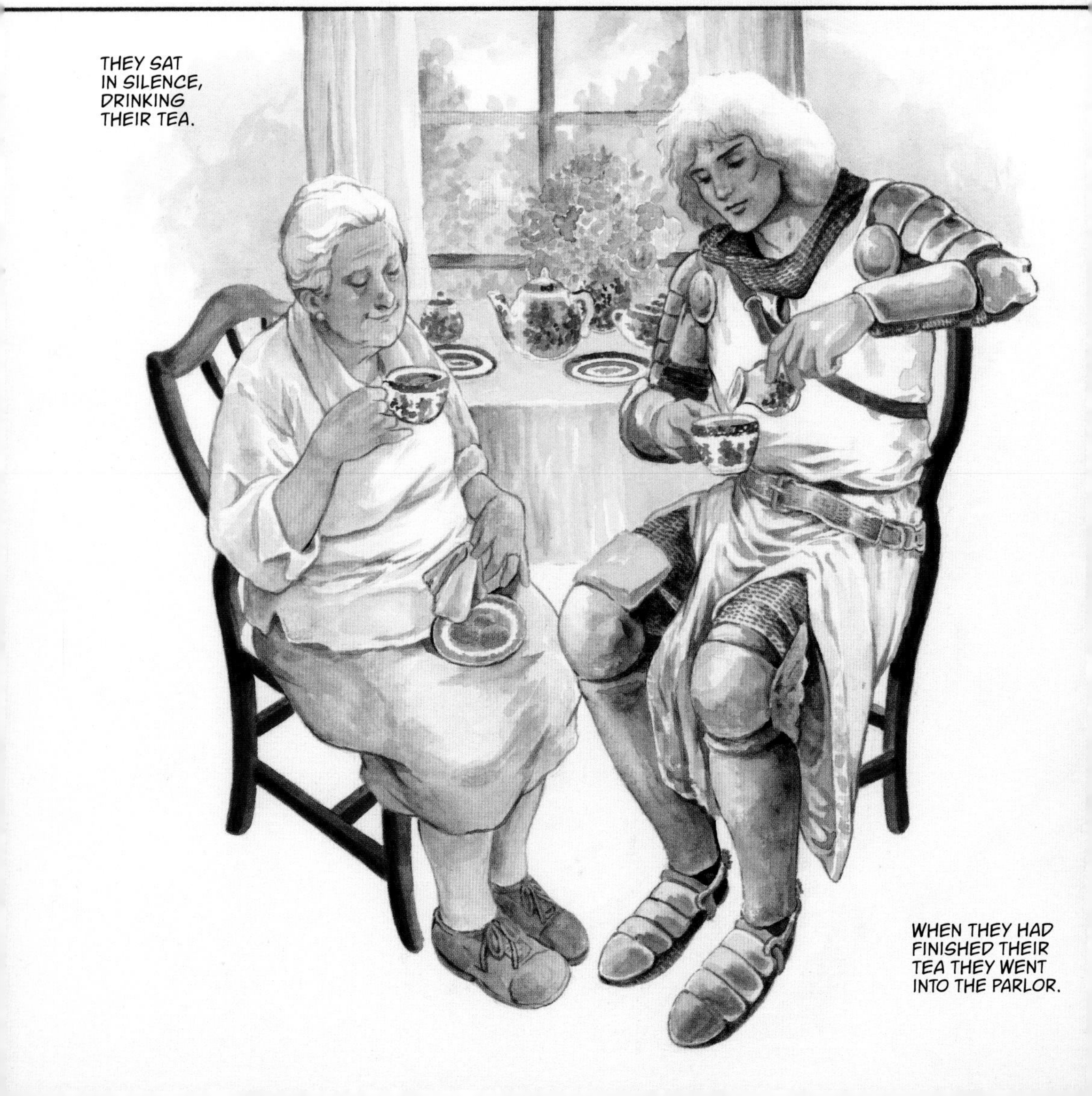
THEY SAT IN SILENCE, DRINKING THEIR TEA.
WHEN THEY HAD FINISHED THEIR TEA THEY WENT INTO THE PARLOR.

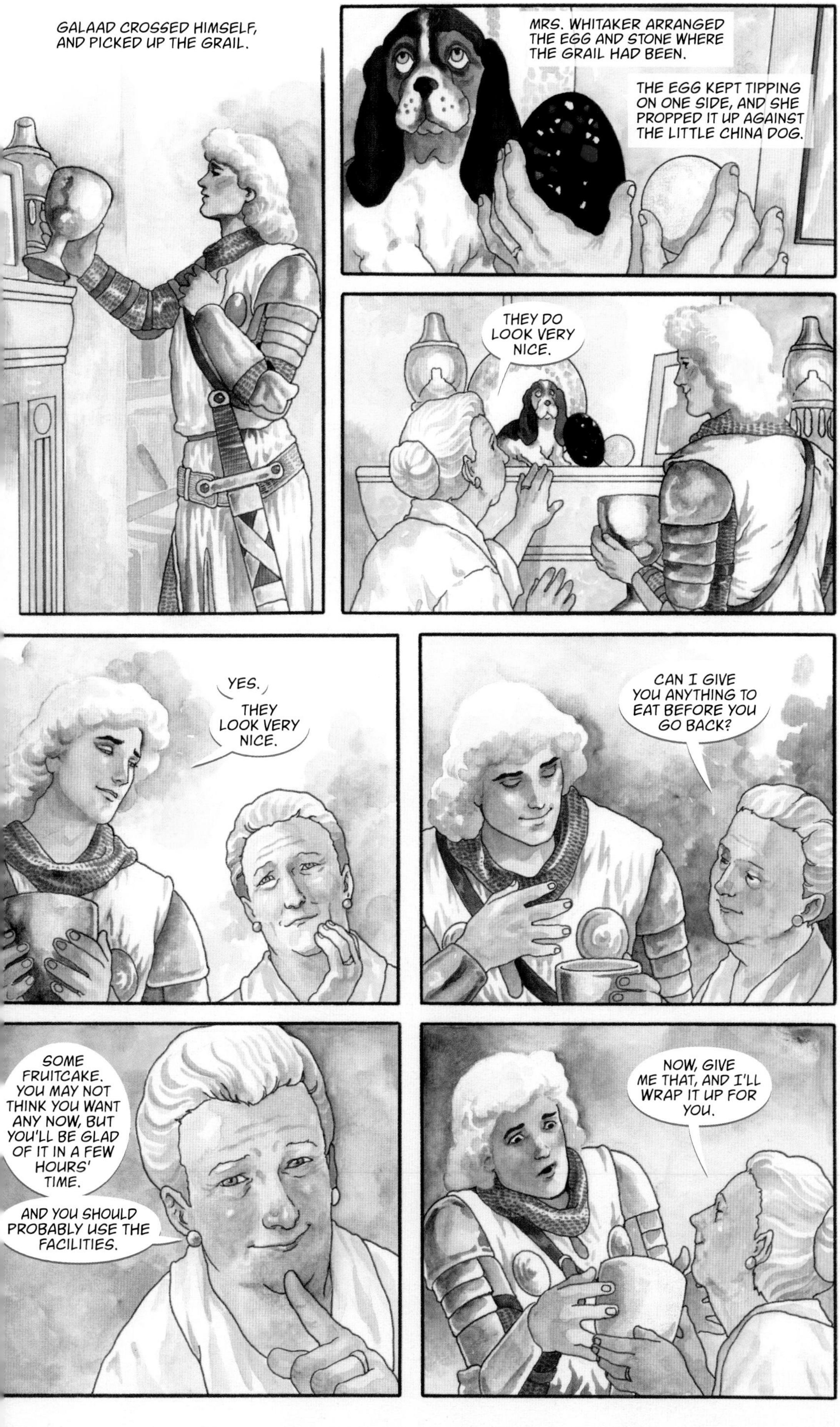
GALAAD CROSSED HIMSELF, AND PICKED UP THE GRAIL.
MRS. WHITAKER ARRANGED THE EGG AND STONE WHERE THE GRAIL HAD BEEN.
THE EGG KEPT TIPPING ON ONE SIDE, AND SHE PROPPED IT UP AGAINST THE LITTLE CHINA DOG.
THEY DO LOOK VERY NICE.
YES.
THEY LOOK VERY NICE.
CAN I GIVE YOU ANYTHING TO EAT BEFORE YOU GO BACK?
SOME FRUITCAKE. YOU MAY NOT THINK YOU WANT ANY NOW, BUT YOU'LL BE GLAD OF IT IN A FEW HOURS' TIME.
AND YOU SHOULD PROBABLY USE THE FACILITIES.
NOW, GIVE ME THAT, AND I'LL WRAP IT UP FOR YOU.

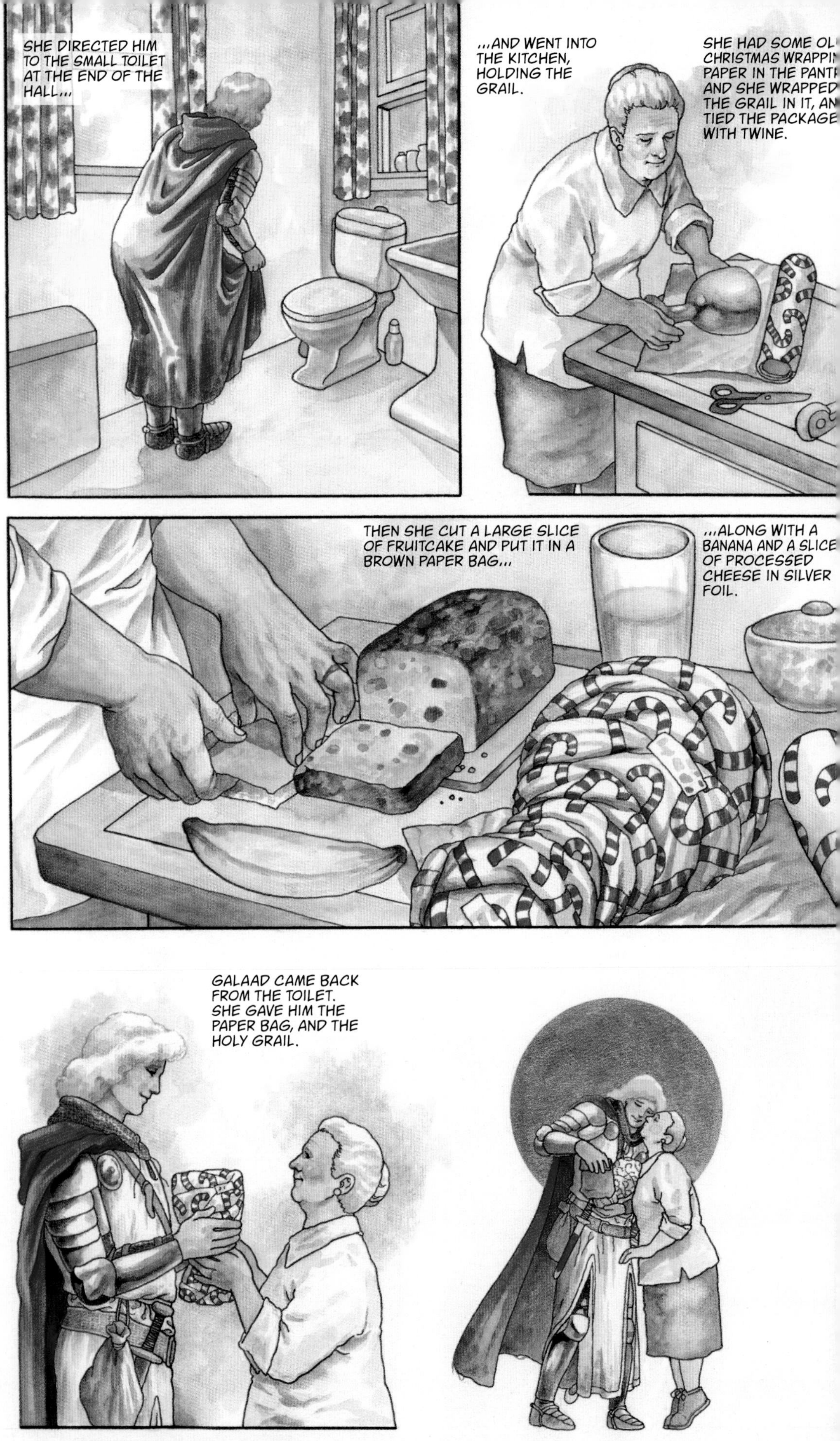
SHE DIRECTED HIM TO THE SMALL TOILET AT THE END OF THE HALL...
...AND WENT INTO THE KITCHEN, HOLDING THE GRAIL.
SHE HAD SOME OL CHRISTMAS WRAPPI PAPER IN THE PANT AND SHE WRAPPED THE GRAIL IN IT, AN TIED THE PACKAGE WITH TWINE.
THEN SHE CUT A LARGE SLICE OF FRUITCAKE AND PUT IT IN A BROWN PAPER BAG...
...ALONG WITH A BANANA AND A SLICE OF PROCESSED CHEESE IN SILVER FOIL.
GALAAD CAME BACK FROM THE TOILET. SHE GAVE HIM THE PAPER BAG, AND THE HOLY GRAIL.

YOU'RE A NICE BOY.

YOU TAKE CARE OF YOURSELF.

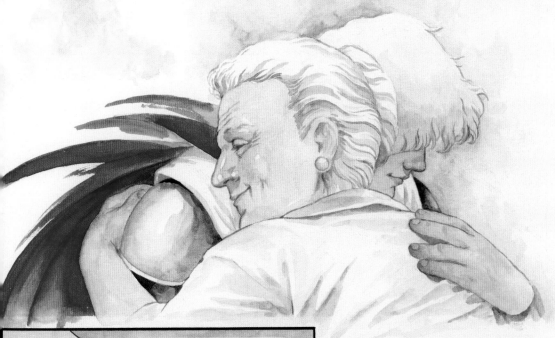

MRS. WHITAKER SHOOED HIM OUT OF THE KITCHEN, AND OUT THE BACK DOOR...

...AND SHE SHUT THE DOOR BEHIND HIM.

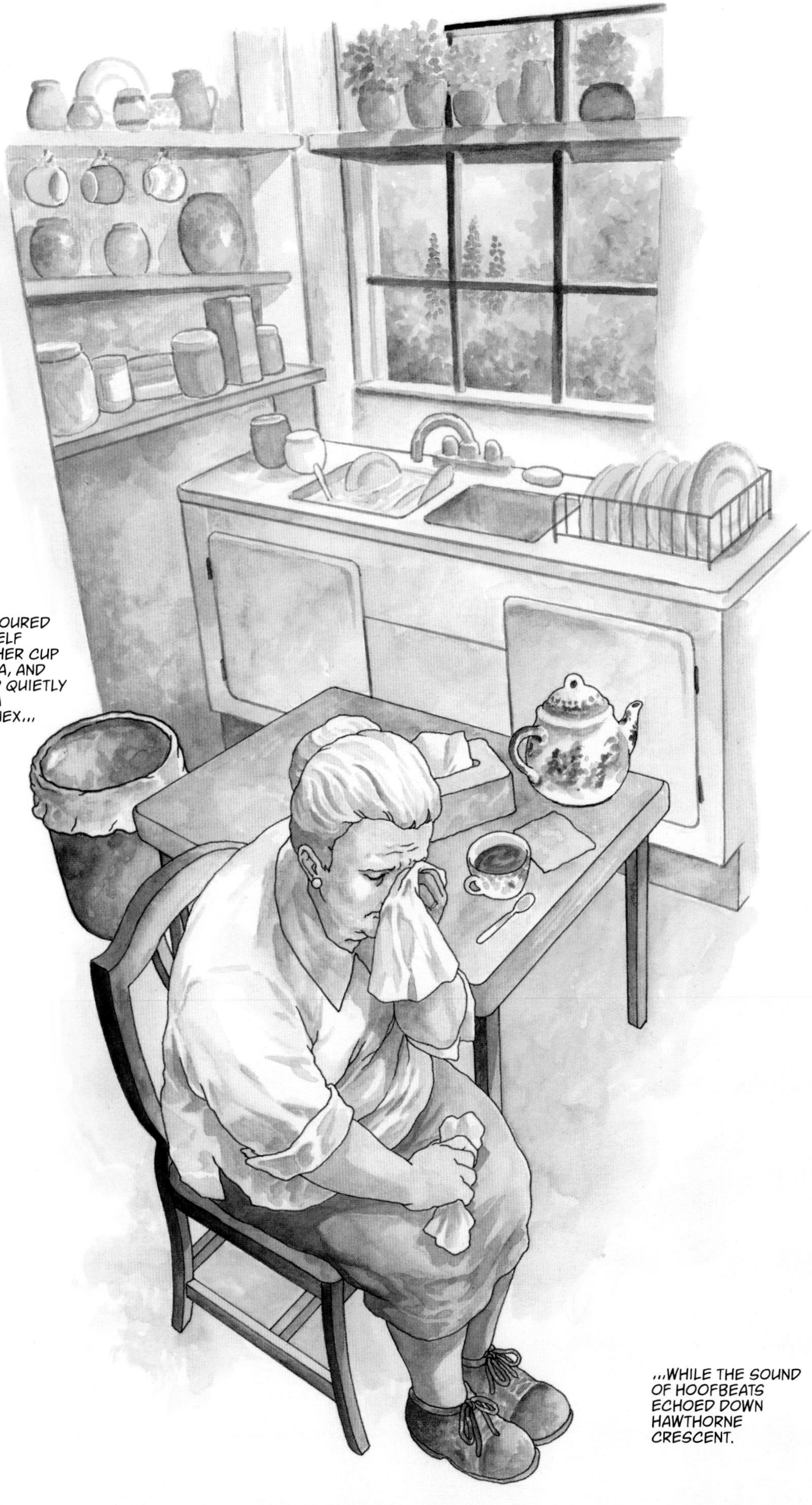
SHE POURED HERSELF ANOTHER CUP OF TEA, AND CRIED QUIETLY INTO A KLEENEX...
...WHILE THE SOUND OF HOOFBEATS ECHOED DOWN HAWTHORNE CRESCENT.

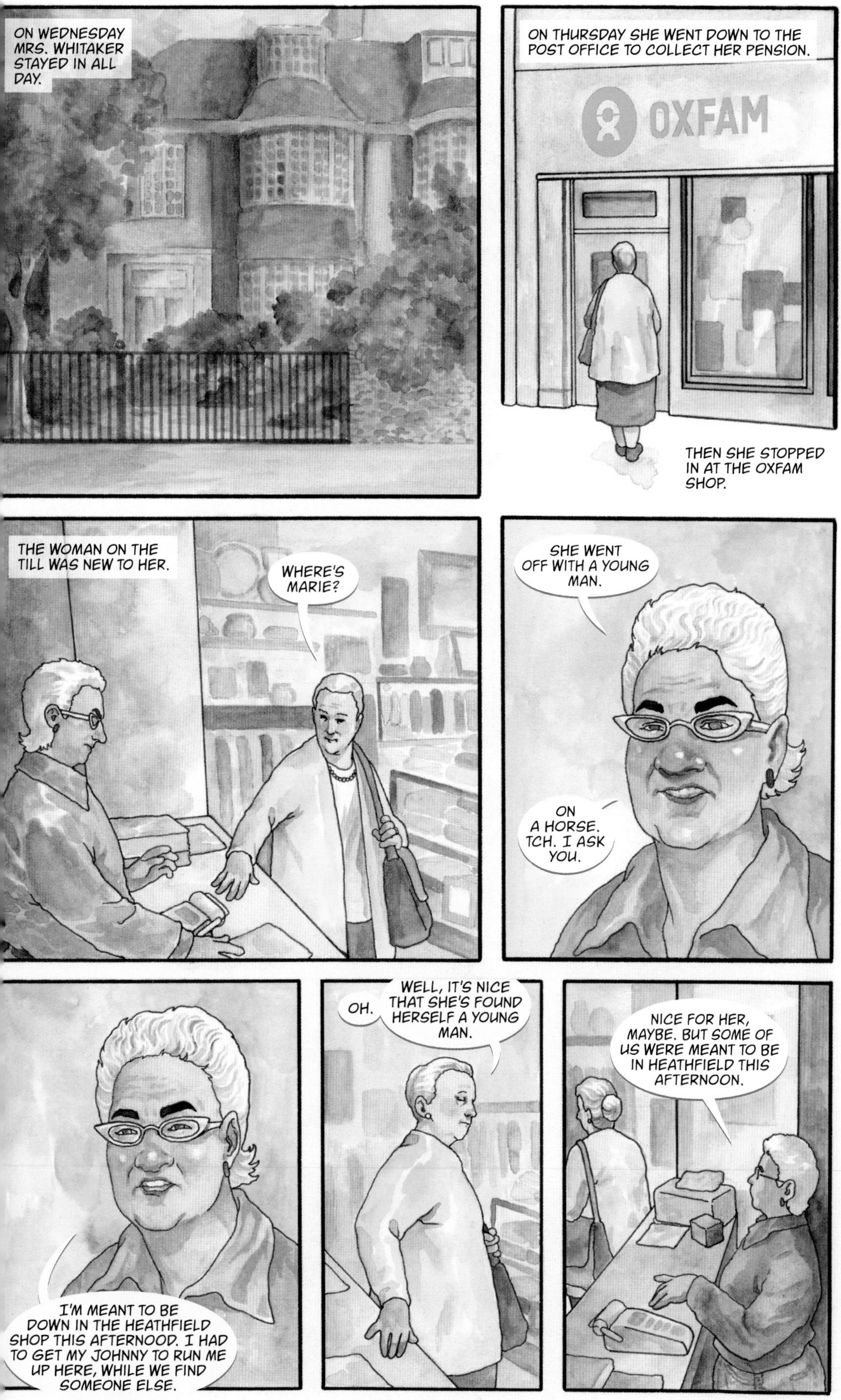

ON WEDNESDAY MRS. WHITAKER STAYED IN ALL DAY.
ON THURSDAY SHE WENT DOWN TO THE POST OFFICE TO COLLECT HER PENSION.
OXFAM
THEN SHE STOPPED IN AT THE OXFAM SHOP.
THE WOMAN ON THE TILL WAS NEW TO HER.
WHERE'S MARIE?
SHE WENT OFF WITH A YOUNG MAN.
ON A HORSE. TCH. I ASK YOU.
I'M MEANT TO BE DOWN IN THE HEATHFIELD SHOP THIS AFTERNOOD. I HAD TO GET MY JOHNNY TO RUN ME UP HERE, WHILE WE FIND SOMEONE ELSE.
OH.
WELL, IT'S NICE THAT SHE'S FOUND HERSELF A YOUNG MAN.
NICE FOR HER, MAYBE. BUT SOME OF US WERE MEANT TO BE IN HEATHFIELD THIS AFTERNOON.

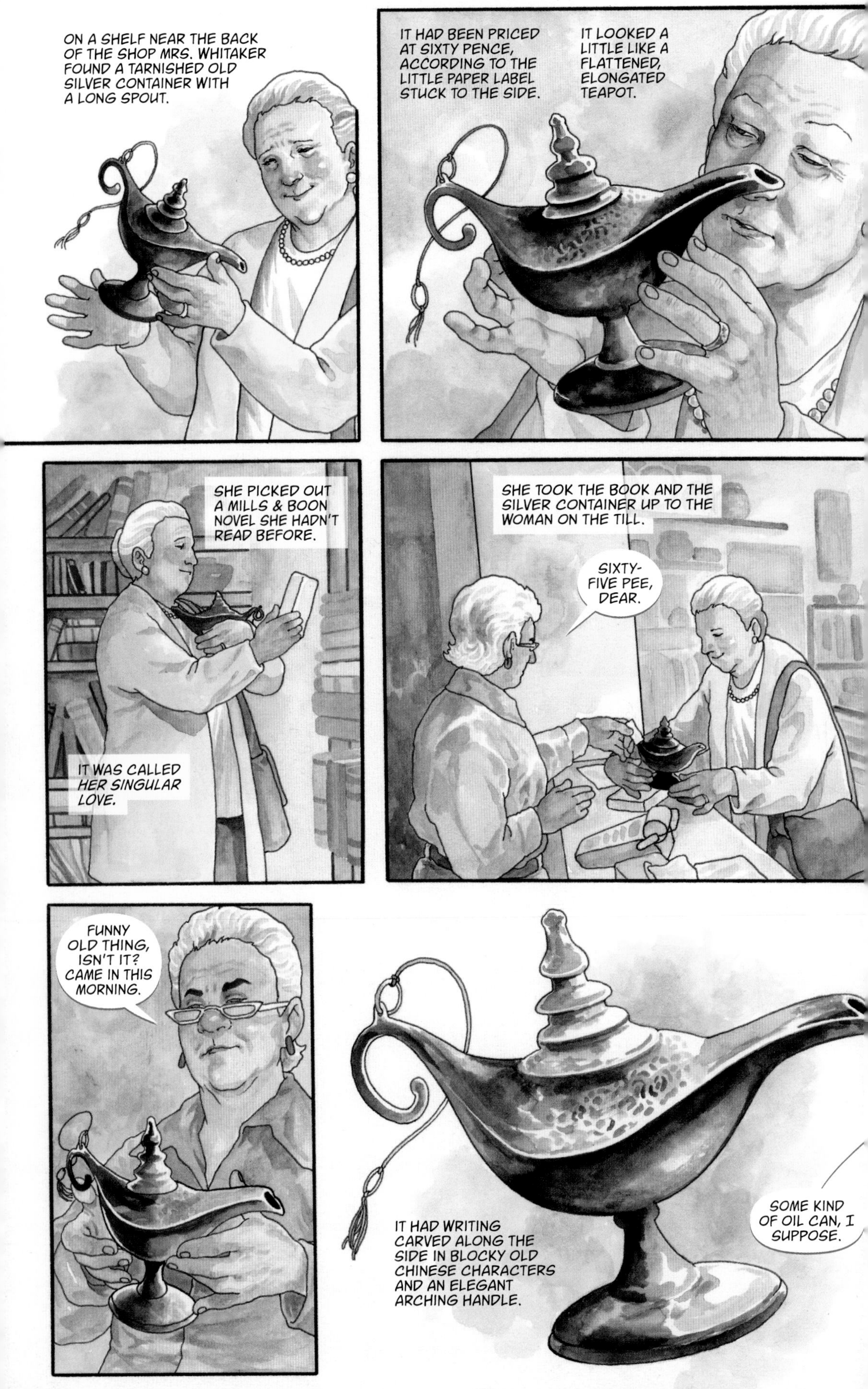

ON A SHELF NEAR THE BACK OF THE SHOP MRS. WHITAKER FOUND A TARNISHED OLD SILVER CONTAINER WITH A LONG SPOUT.
IT HAD BEEN PRICED AT SIXTY PENCE, ACCORDING TO THE LITTLE PAPER LABEL STUCK TO THE SIDE.
IT LOOKED A LITTLE LIKE A FLATTENED, ELONGATED TEAPOT.
SHE PICKED OUT A MILLS & BOON NOVEL SHE HADN'T READ BEFORE.
IT WAS CALLED *HER SINGULAR LOVE.*
SHE TOOK THE BOOK AND THE SILVER CONTAINER UP TO THE WOMAN ON THE TILL.
SIXTY-FIVE PEE, DEAR.
FUNNY OLD THING, ISN'T IT? CAME IN THIS MORNING.
IT HAD WRITING CARVED ALONG THE SIDE IN BLOCKY OLD CHINESE CHARACTERS AND AN ELEGANT ARCHING HANDLE.
SOME KIND OF OIL CAN, I SUPPOSE.

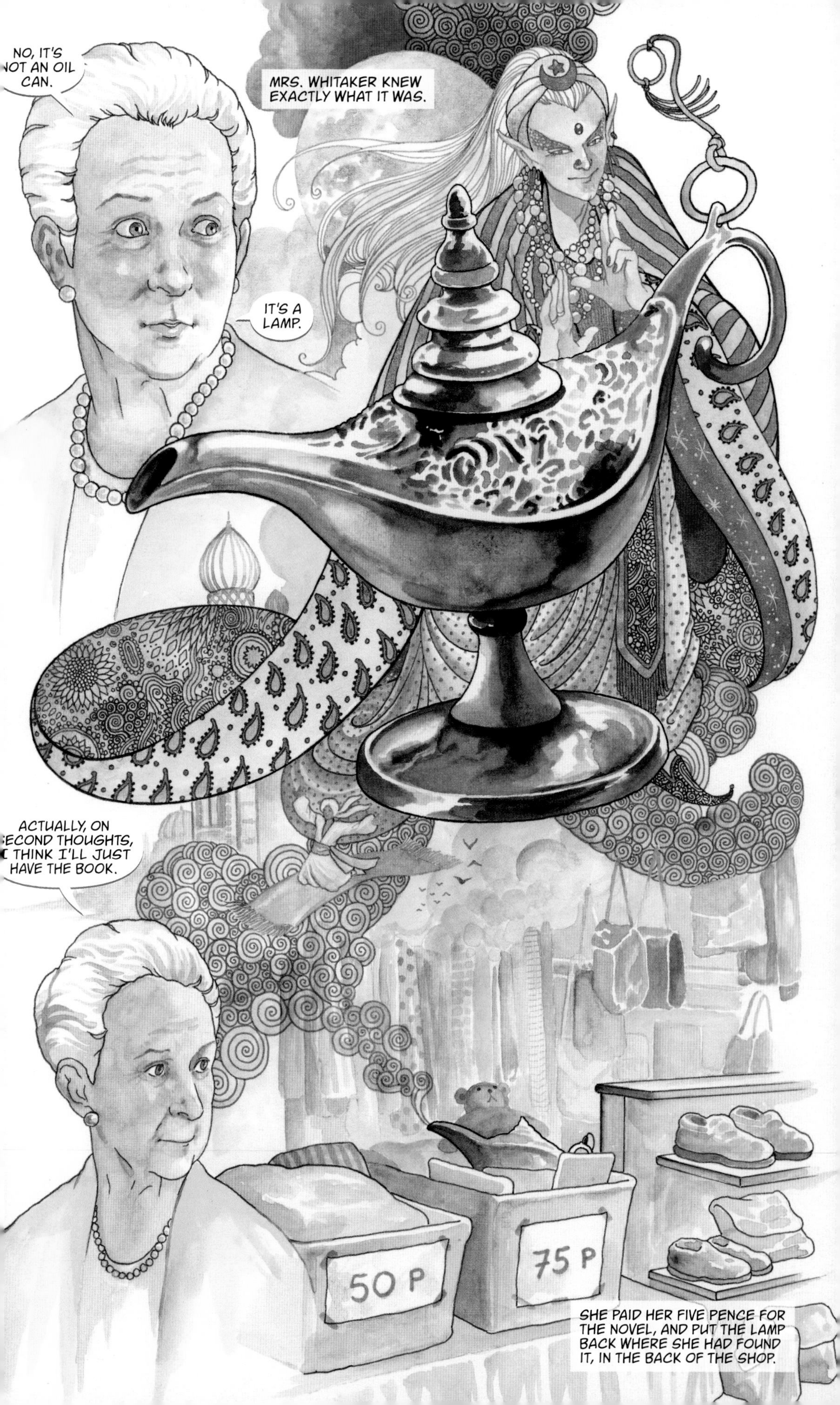

NO, IT'S NOT AN OIL CAN.
MRS. WHITAKER KNEW EXACTLY WHAT IT WAS.
IT'S A LAMP.
ACTUALLY, ON SECOND THOUGHTS, I THINK I'LL JUST HAVE THE BOOK.
50 P
75 P
SHE PAID HER FIVE PENCE FOR THE NOVEL, AND PUT THE LAMP BACK WHERE SHE HAD FOUND IT, IN THE BACK OF THE SHOP.

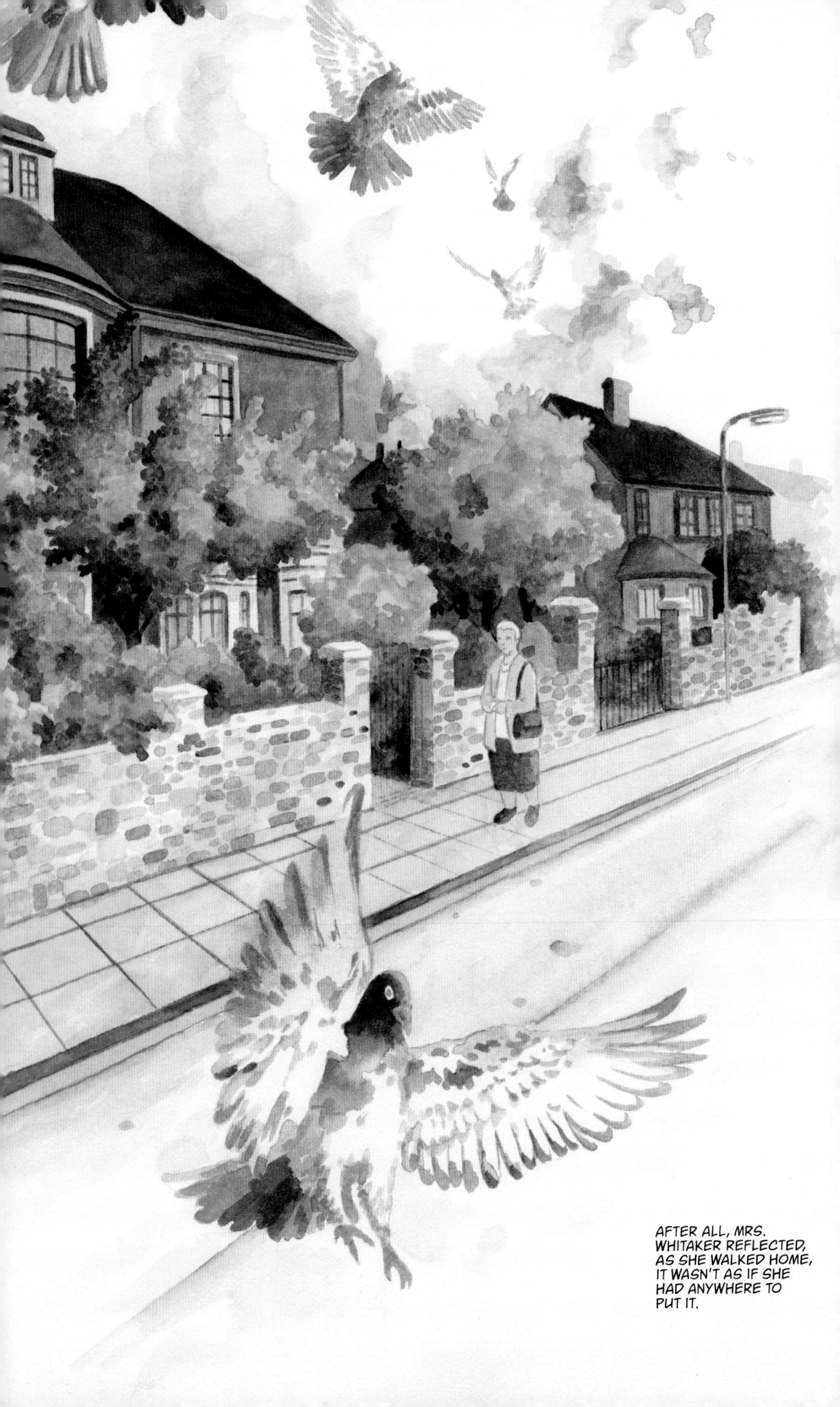
AFTER ALL, MRS. WHITAKER REFLECTED, AS SHE WALKED HOME, IT WASN'T AS IF SHE HAD ANYWHERE TO PUT IT.

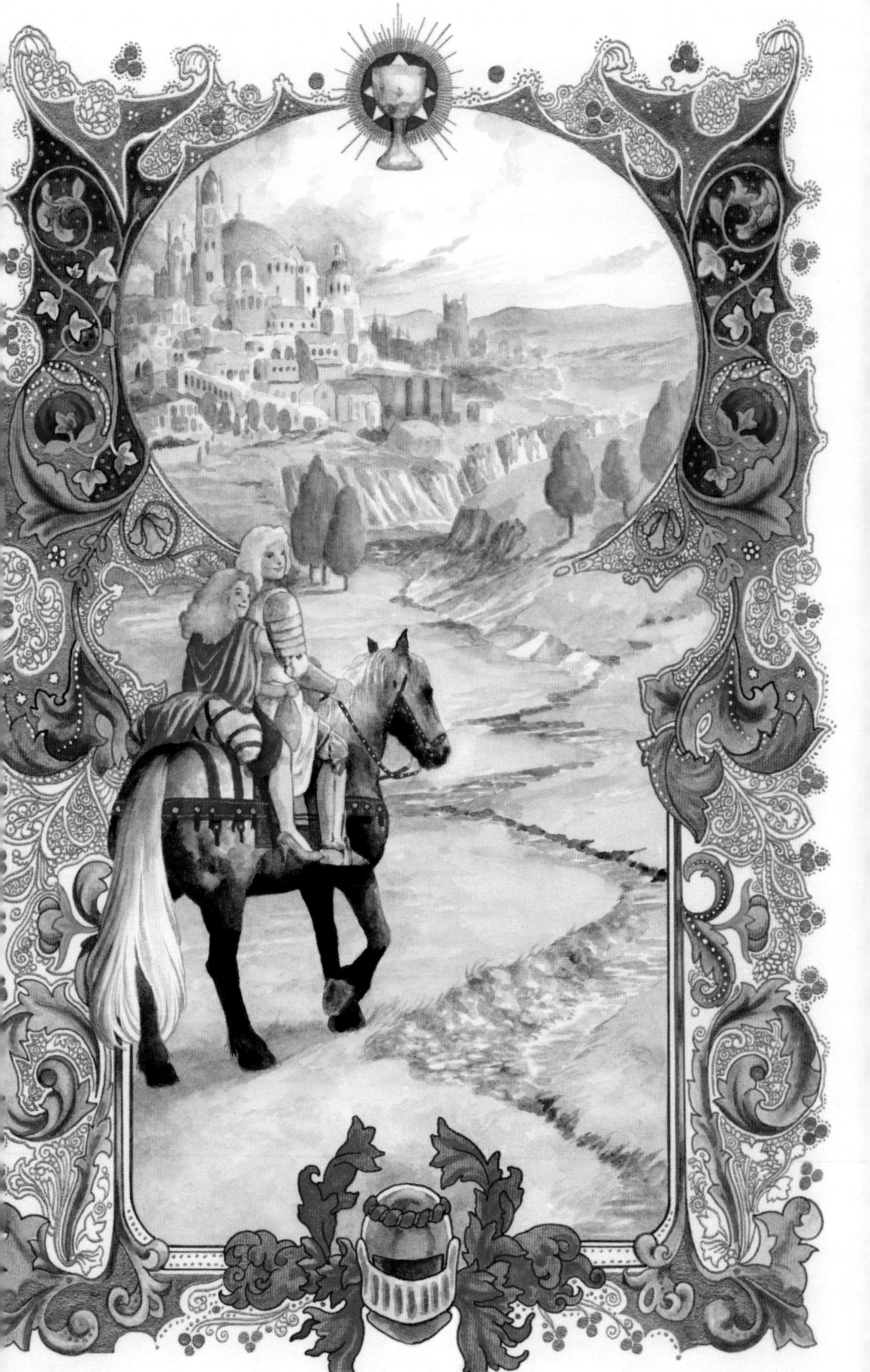

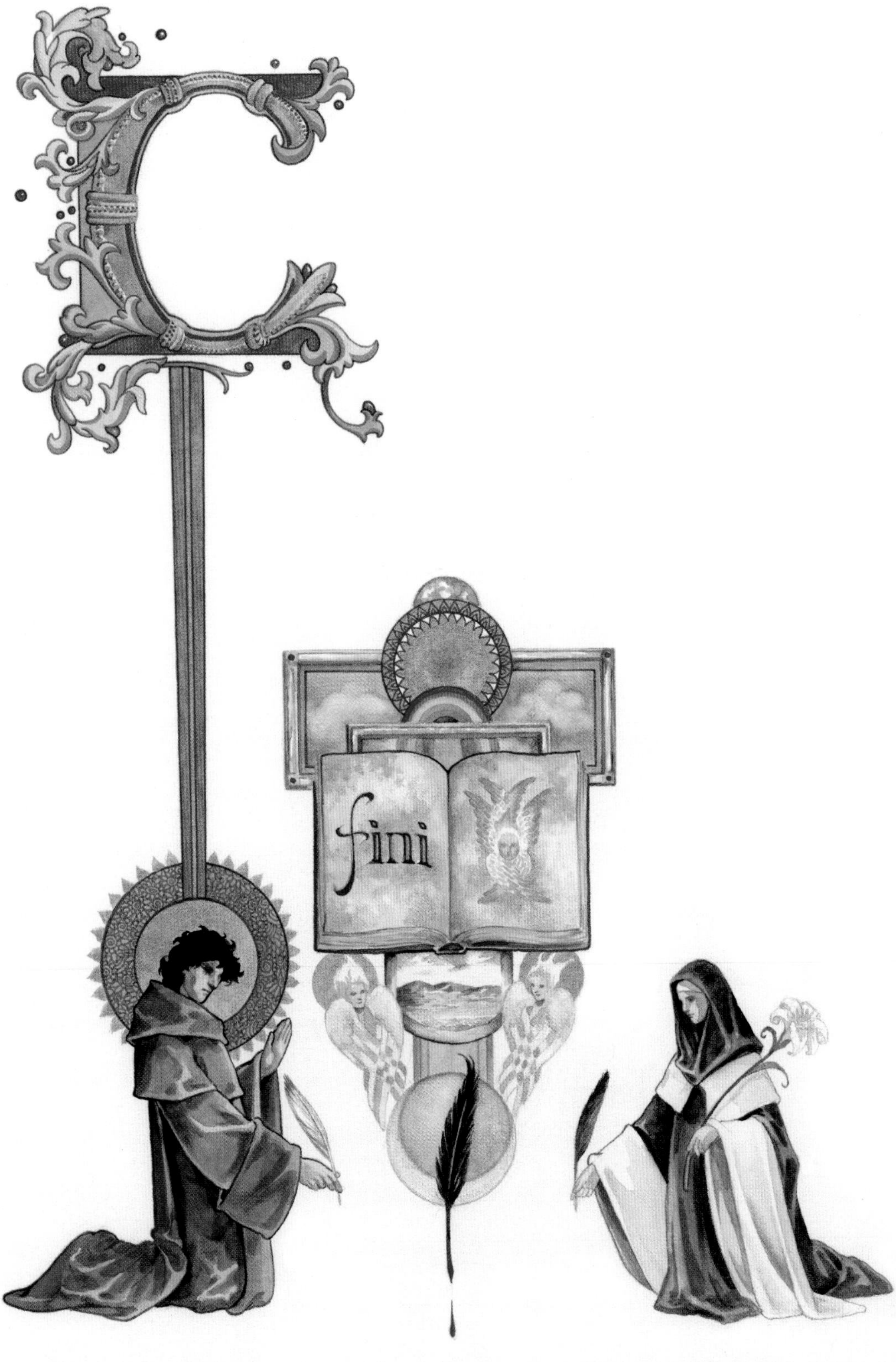
fini

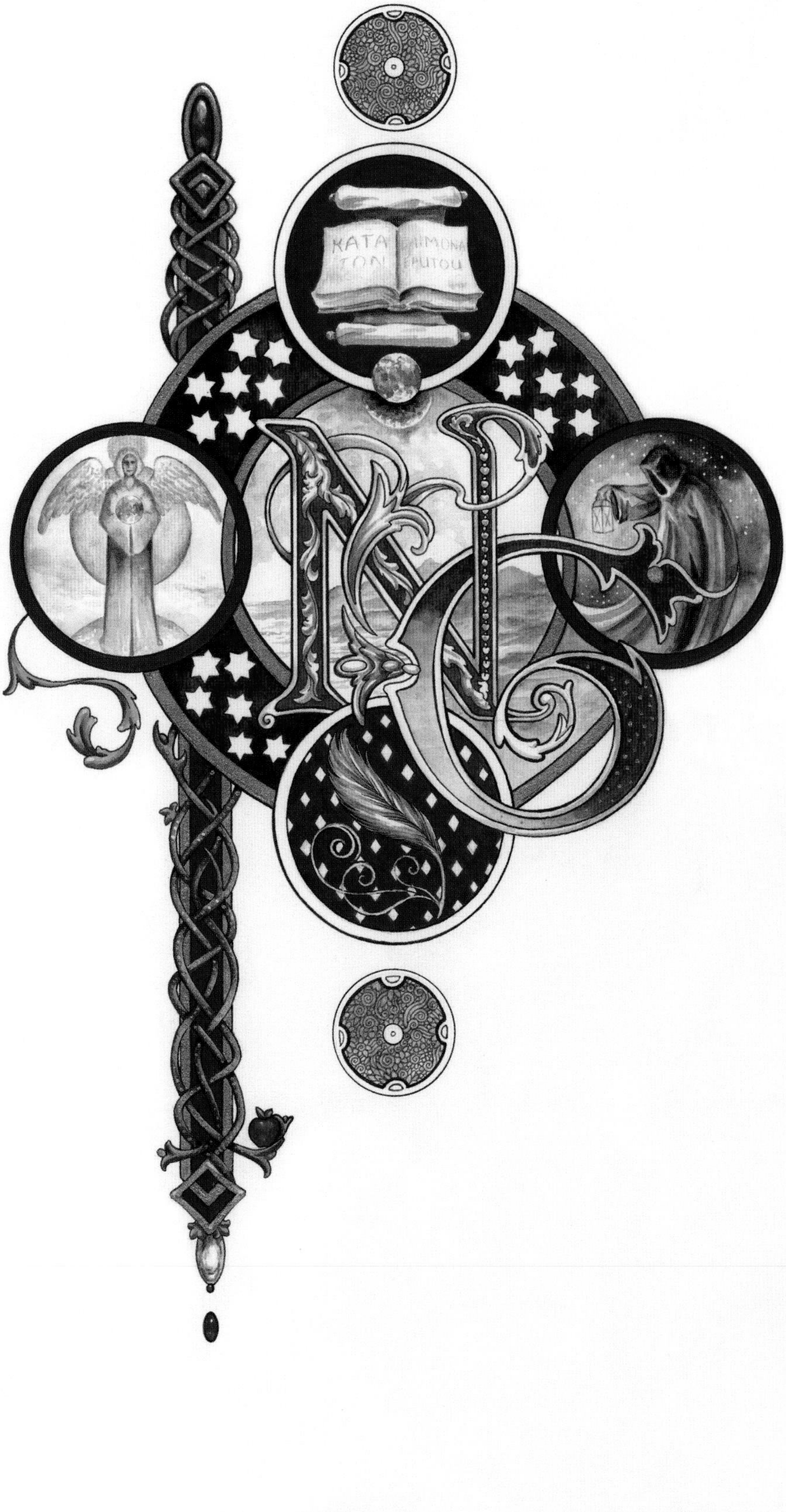
KATA
TON

Orate Pro Pictura

CHIVALRY

❖

NOTES

In those days of yore before Neil Gaiman got very, very famous, the most amazing new stories would come whirring through my fax machine, usually around 1 a.m. when it was God knows what time in the UK, and I would read every tale with greedy enthusiasm.

But when I read "Chivalry," I loved it so much it made my heart ache.

I spent the next several decades pursuing this project like the Holy Grail quest it was. When I achieved it, I had massive doubts about whether or not I was worthy of it, and only the good readers may be the judge of that worthiness based on what they now hold in their hands.

I've been an Arthuriana enthusiast since I was about ten years old, after I found a *Reader's Digest Best Loved Books for Young Readers* edition of Howard Pyle's *The Tale of King Arthur and His Knights* illustrated by Darrell Sweet tucked in the library of a wealthy family friend. I used to go and hide behind the armchair by the big window there and read for hours and avoid people. I wanted a copy of this book of my very own so badly I even considered stealing it.

But that would be unworthy, so I didn't.

I spent many years trying to track down a copy in the days before the internet made finding books easy. I discovered the complete four-volume Howard Pyle edition of Arthurian tales at the public library, and spent the next several decades on a mission to collect every single book about King Arthur in existence. This mission eventually became kind of ridiculous. I realized I just didn't like most of the novels especially, and I finally sold off much of the library.

But I still have my Howard Pyle books, and my illustrated editions by N.C. Wyeth, and oh, so many books about the Holy Grail.

When I read "Chivalry," I knew exactly how I wanted to do the art and would periodically bug Neil about the prospect of getting the graphic novel adaptation gig. Unfortunately, a Hollywood producer had the rights tied up, and it took over twenty-five years to free them from his clutches.

When I finally did get the go-ahead, I cried with joy. Then I had a breakdown and could barely function for months, not only paralyzed by the world situation and COVID woes, but after spending many years with plans for the story whirring in my head, I realized many of my goals were simply unworkable.

I'd fan fictioned a lot of the tale in such a way that I'd let my inner mind version of the work stray from Neil's thematic intent.

I'd hoped to create the book, start to finish, as a genuine illuminated manuscript. I put months of effort into learning to work on parchment and to master the difficult raised gold leaf technique, which ate up a huge amount of my lead time on this project, and my editor would like to hold me responsible for some of his grey hairs.

Not only would the parchment end up costing almost as much as I was getting paid to do the art, but months of experimentation with process, training, and scanning the art for print eventually convinced me that virtually all the techniques I wanted to use would be lost in translation. The raised gold technique was completely unworkable, real gold tends to print as brown, the translucent quality of parchment is lost entirely, and the project might even bankrupt me if I wasn't careful, aside from taking, maybe 3–5 years to do it as I really wanted to do it. I hoped to scan every page for print then bind it into one complete illuminated manuscript, and wouldn't that be cool.

My inspiration for the art on "Chivalry" was Alberto Sangorski, a little known calligrapher and illustrator born in 1862. Sangorski did an illuminated manuscript edition of Tennyson's *Le Morte d'Arthur* that I stumbled upon by pure luck one day, having never heard of it when I found it.

In preinternet days, that might qualify as a miracle.

On my previous major projects for Neil Gaiman such as *Troll Bridge*, we barely spoke at all. And while we both knew I wanted to adapt the look of Irish Arts and Crafts master Harry Clarke's work for *Snow, Glass, Apples*, again, we didn't talk much. I had free reign.

However, we did go over many aspects of "Chivalry." Not only did I realize much of the story was very personal to Neil, but the Sangorski approach I wanted to take was just too stolid and serious for what should be a light, comedic tale. I'd spent entirely too much time ruminating on a project that I wanted to meld the mediums of illuminated manuscript and comics, and not enough time trying to figure out what the story really was. I don't

want free reign more than I want the story to be right.

So it was back to the drawing board.

Another challenge on this project was COVID, and not just the general world horror of it, but the fact that I could not get out and do the research I intended to do for the work. The "Chivalry" house and town are real places, and normally I'd get on a plane and take 3,427 pictures for reference. But like everyone else, I was stuck in my home.

Many, oh, so many hours on the internet later, I went down the research rabbit hole way more than I needed to, because that's how I roll. While Neil couldn't remember the address, I was able to find the street where Mrs. Whitaker lived, using an image search map, and we went down that street until Neil spotted the house. Then I was able to find a fourteen-year-old real estate listing that included awesomely hideous interior photos featuring ugly paint and a bean-bag chair.

We even had a tea-pot audition where I took many photos of my collection, settling on the Brown Betty and my cherished antique Blue Willow.

My mom served as general model for Mrs. Whitaker. Mom is rather too slender and youthful looking, so I made some tweaks, but young Mrs. Whitaker is a perfect portrait of my mom. Dad is Mr. Whitaker.

Thank you, Mom and Dad. For everything.

Young me is Marie. I finally get my knight in shining armor.

I regret to inform everyone, Sir Galahad does not exist. He somewhat resembles an old boyfriend who passed away in 1989, and

I also use the character in my space opera series *A Distant Soil*. He looks pretty much here in *Chivalry* as he does there.

While I was able to bring aspects of Sangorski's work to the illuminated manuscript segments of Chivalry, I decided to take a different approach to the rest of the art. I wanted the work to have a heartwarming, comfortable feel, so I modeled my watercolors on the works of illustrator Beatrix Potter, with their mellow golds and greens and naturalist approach.

I haven't even tried to hand paint a comic book since 1991, and not having done any large scale watercolor works in years, this was a challenge. I was so unsure of my ability in the beginning, I did several alternate versions of pages—and the cover—in pen and ink just in case I would have to ditch the watercolor entirely and go for digital color.

Most of the figure work was done from imagination. In keeping with the comedic feel of the story, I wanted a slightly cartoon-ish approach to the people. I shifted to a more highly rendered and realized approach in illuminated manuscript sections as if we were blinking in and out from one world to the next.

Hope that works for you.

In addition to Sangorski's work, I was influenced by the art of British Arts and Crafts artist Jessie Bayes, who worked in a wide variety of media, but whose delicate illuminated manuscripts are not in print anywhere. You can find scans of some of her work online, as you can the works of Sangorski. Some of Sangorski's works are in print, but they are a bit pricey. My first action when I got my first check for the work on Chivalry was to go out and buy some.

This is why artists are always broke.

There are also innumerable references to many ancient texts and artists, some of which are unknown or which I can't even identify, but you'll find glancing references to the Pre-Raphaelites, including one panel based on Sir John Everett Millais's "A Dream of the Past: Sir Isumbras at the Ford."

My art is rendered in Daniel Smith watercolors, some of them iridescent, which can't be reproduced as seen by the naked eye. This is intentional. I wanted whoever holds the original art to have something no one else can experience. Before I did the art for the book, I scanned all colors to test color shift until I settled on what I could live with between the original and the final printed work.

I auditioned some eighteen real and faux golds before settling on the final mediums to get the gold effects I wanted in the book. Some are 18K or 24K gold ink or paint. I stumbled upon a digital technique to get it to shine a bit, ditching the flat gold leaf I'd originally intended.

I used Strathmore 500 multimedia board, which takes precise watercolor very well. I also used Faber-Castell inks.

As I write this, I am in the last days of completing the art, and nearly in tears at having taken yet more precious time from finishing the pages, as if all the time I spent doing research I would never use wasn't bad enough.

This entire project has been a struggle between what I think I am worthy of and what I hope to be.

Like the search for the Grail itself.

CHIVALRY

SKETCHBOOK

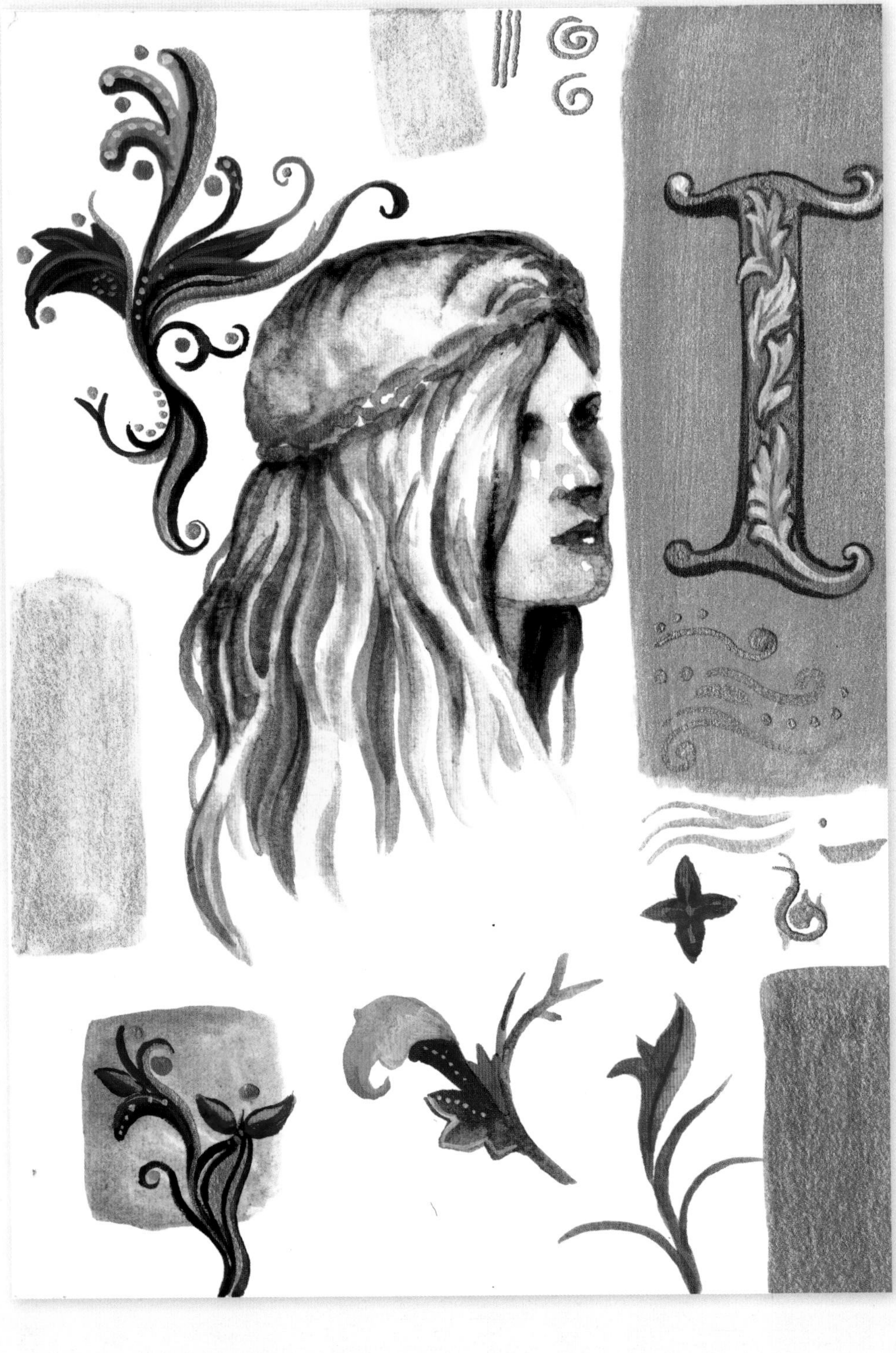

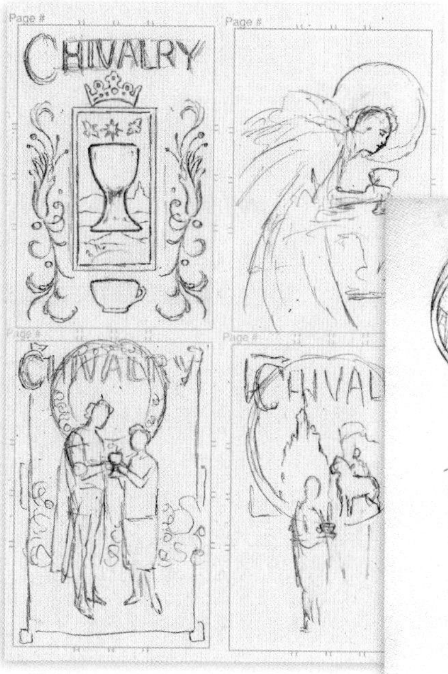
Page #
CHIVALRY
Page #
Page #
Page #

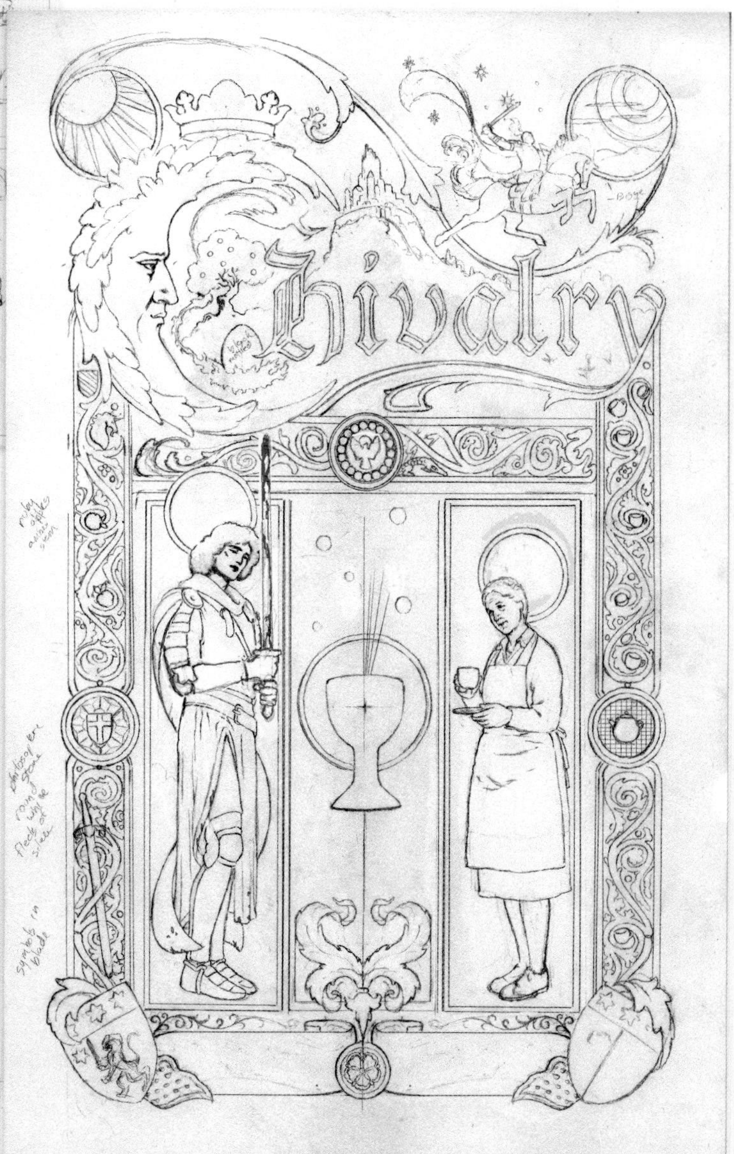

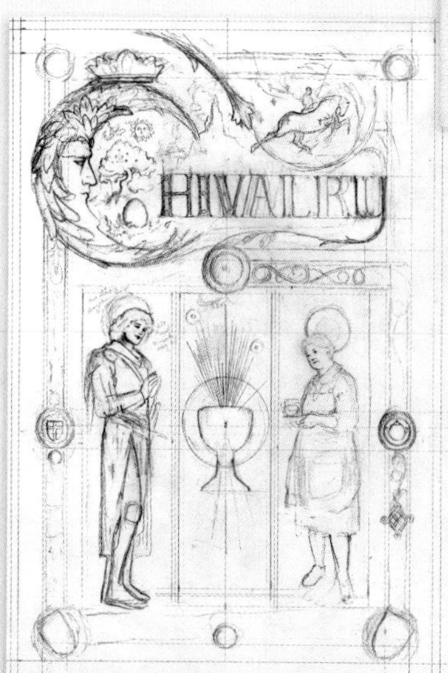

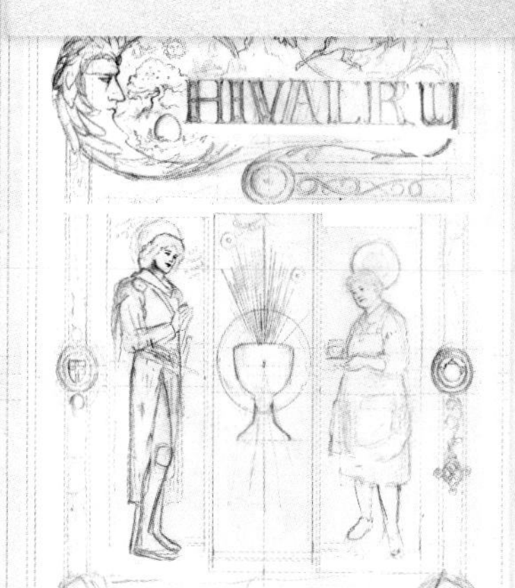

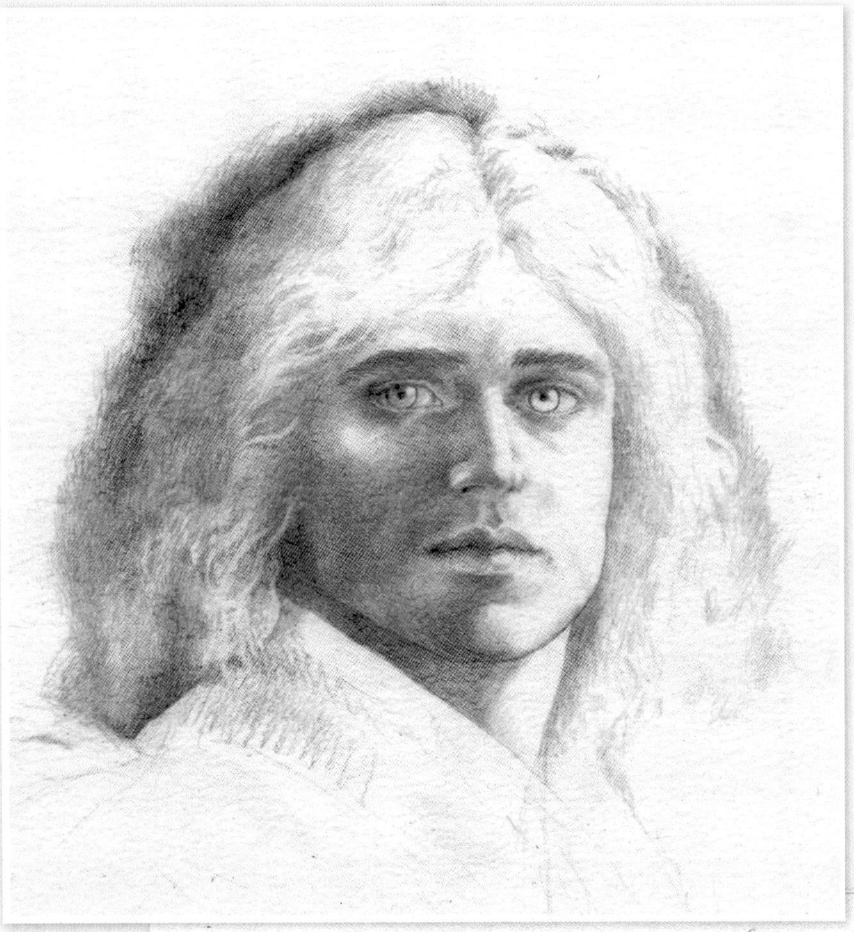

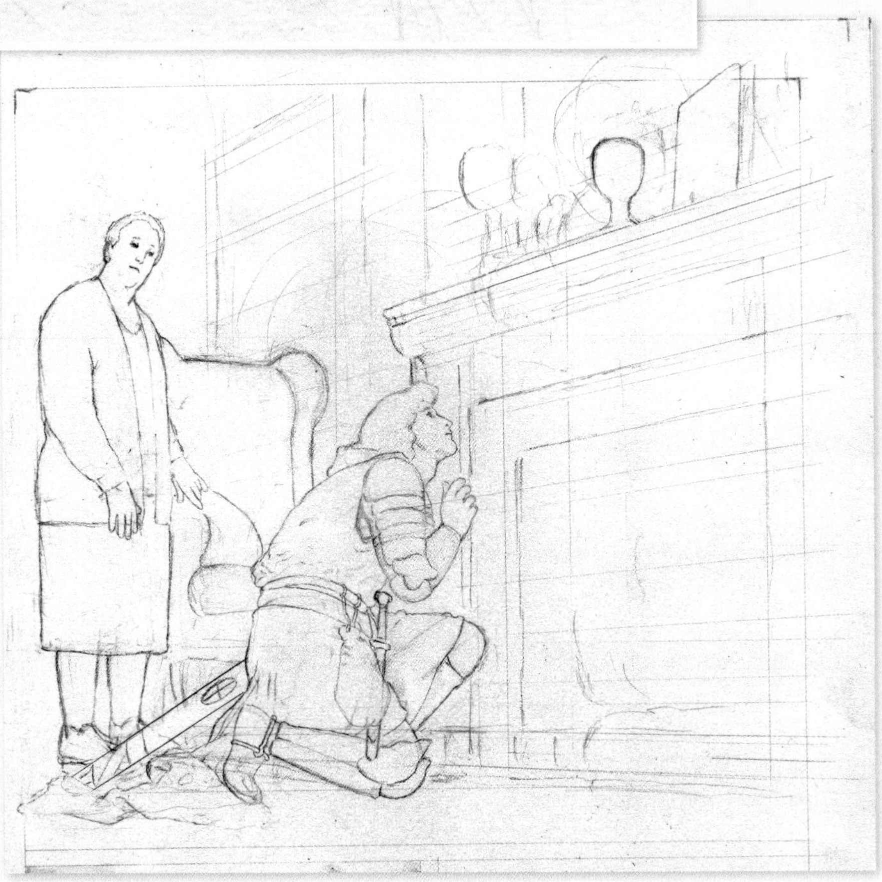

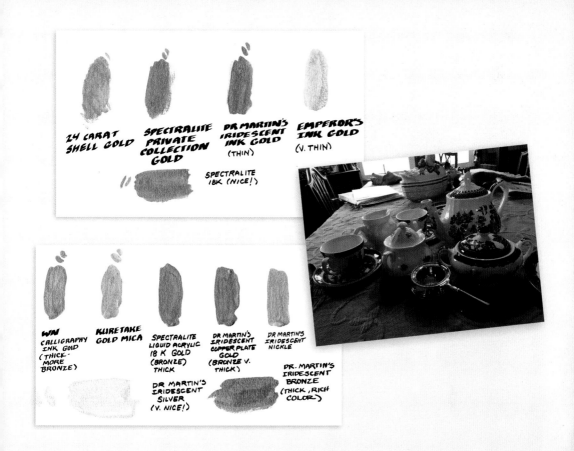

24 CARAT SHELL GOLD
SPECTRALITE PRIVATE COLLECTION GOLD
DR MARTIN'S IRIDESCENT INK GOLD (THIN)
EMPEROR'S INK GOLD (V. THIN)
SPECTRALITE 18K (NICE!)

WN CALLIGRAPHY INK GOLD (THICK - MORE BRONZE)
KURETAKE GOLD MICA
SPECTRALITE LIQUID ACRYLIC 18 K GOLD (BRONZE) THICK
DR MARTIN'S IRIDESCENT COPPER PLATE GOLD (BRONZE V. THICK)
DR MARTIN'S IRIDESCENT NICKLE
DR MARTIN'S IRIDESCENT SILVER (V. NICE!)
DR. MARTIN'S IRIDESCENT BRONZE (THICK, RICH COLOR)

INTERIORS
INTERIORS
DOUBLE PAGE SPREAD: CUT AS SHOWN, ABUT PAGE EDGES, TAPE ON BACK, DO NOT OVERLAP
DOUBLE PAGE SPREAD: CUT AS SHOWN, ABUT PAGE EDGES, TAPE ON BACK, DO NOT OVERLAP

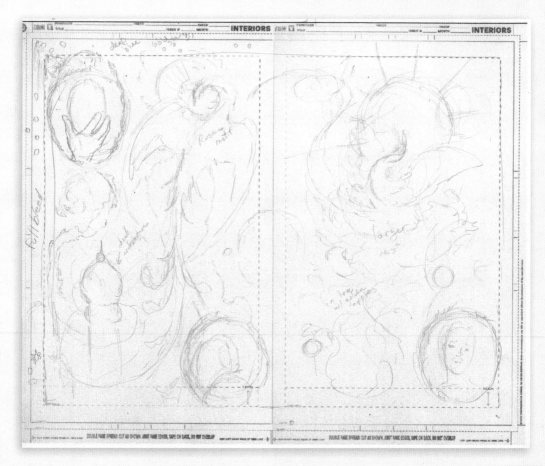

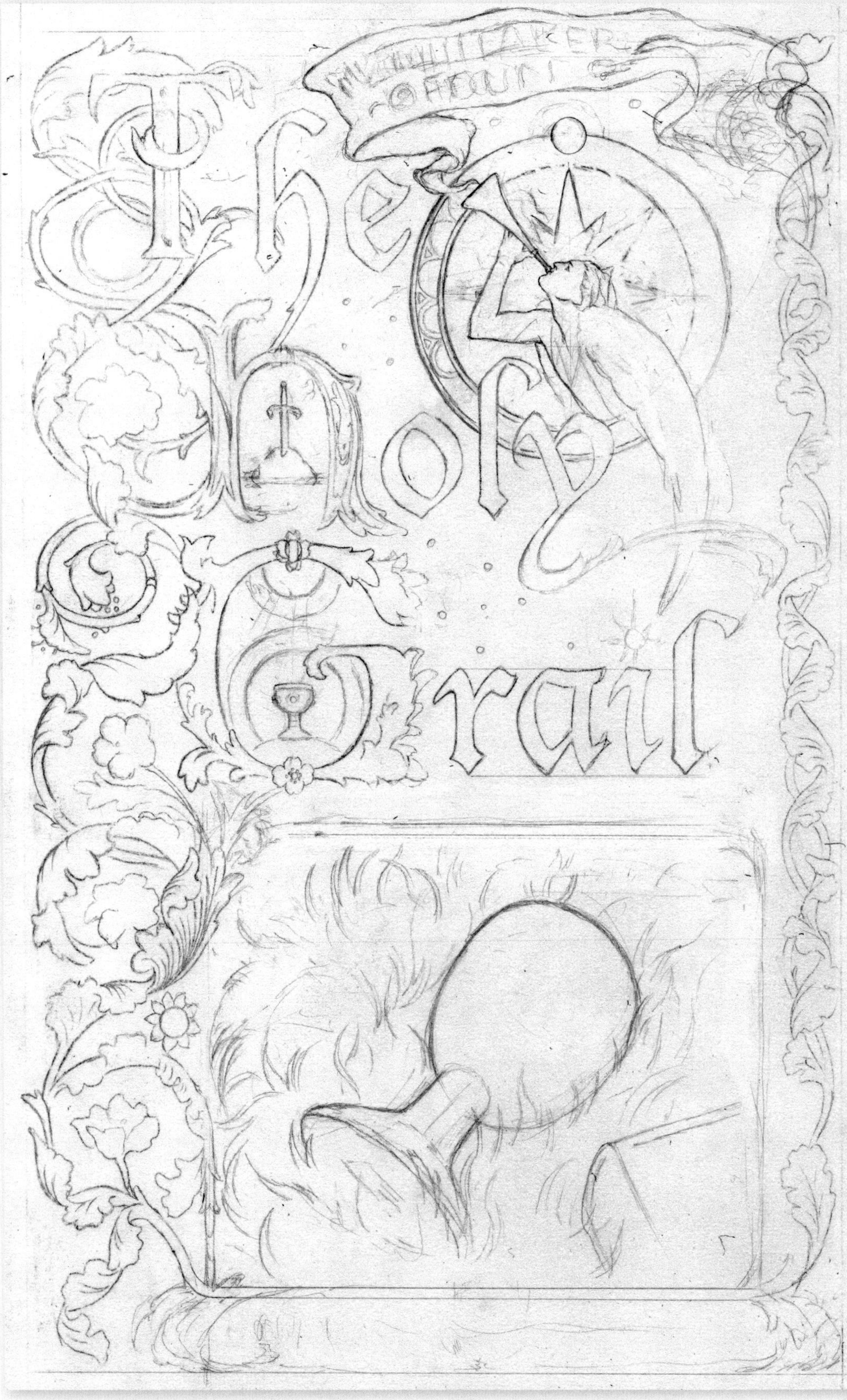
The Holy Grail

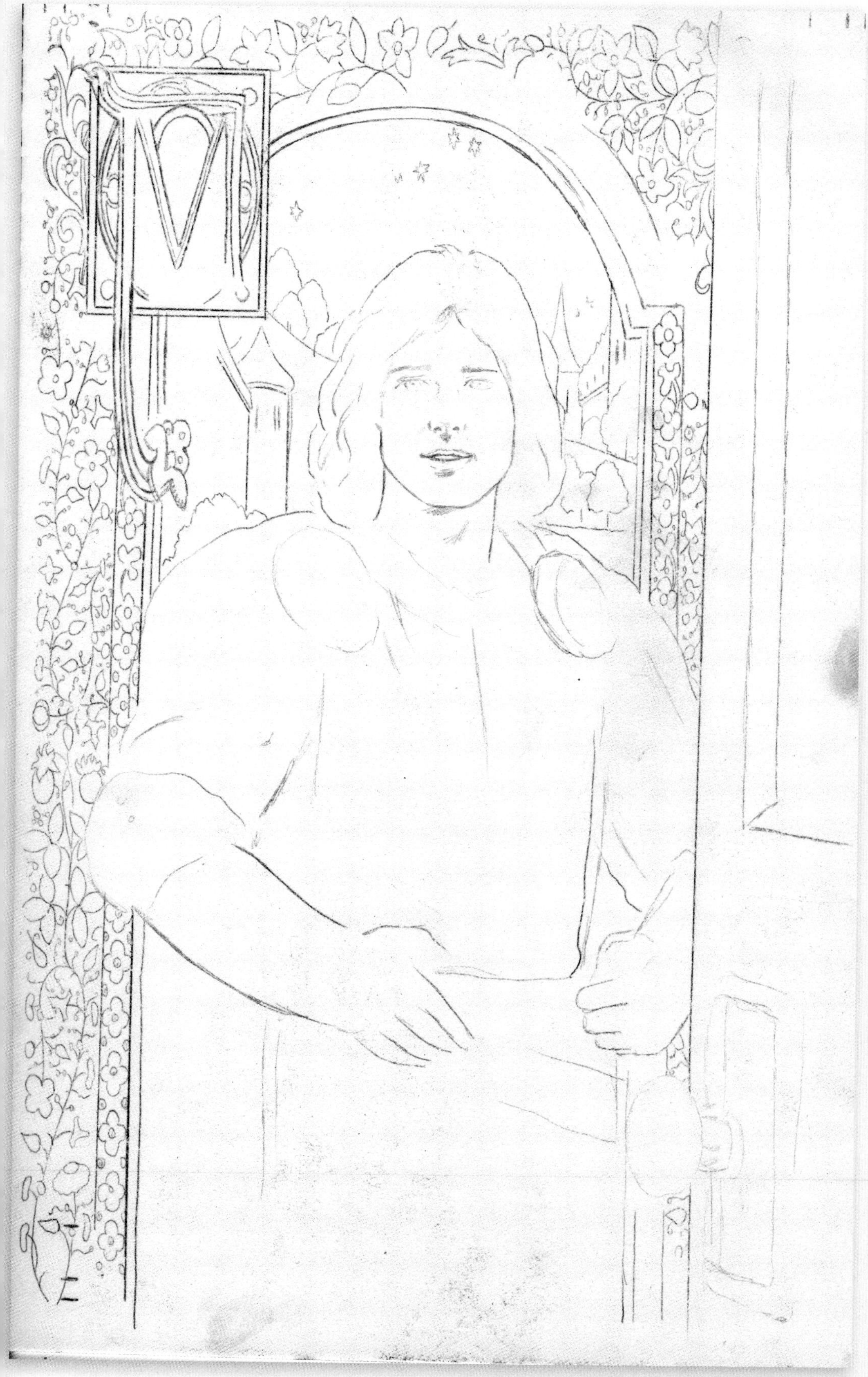

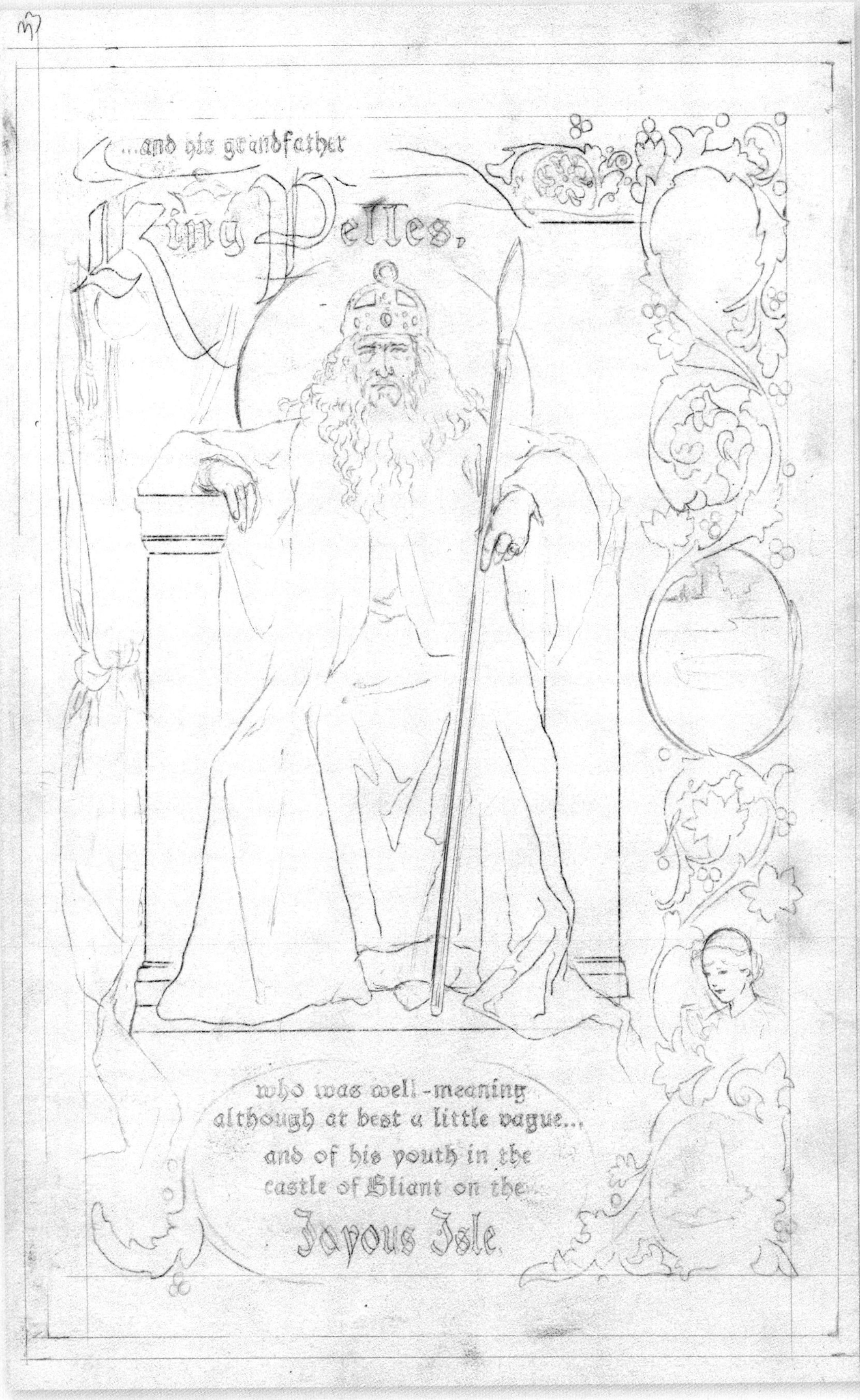
...and his grandfather
King Pelles,
who was well-meaning
although at best a little vague...
and of his youth in the
castle of Bliant on the
Joyous Isle

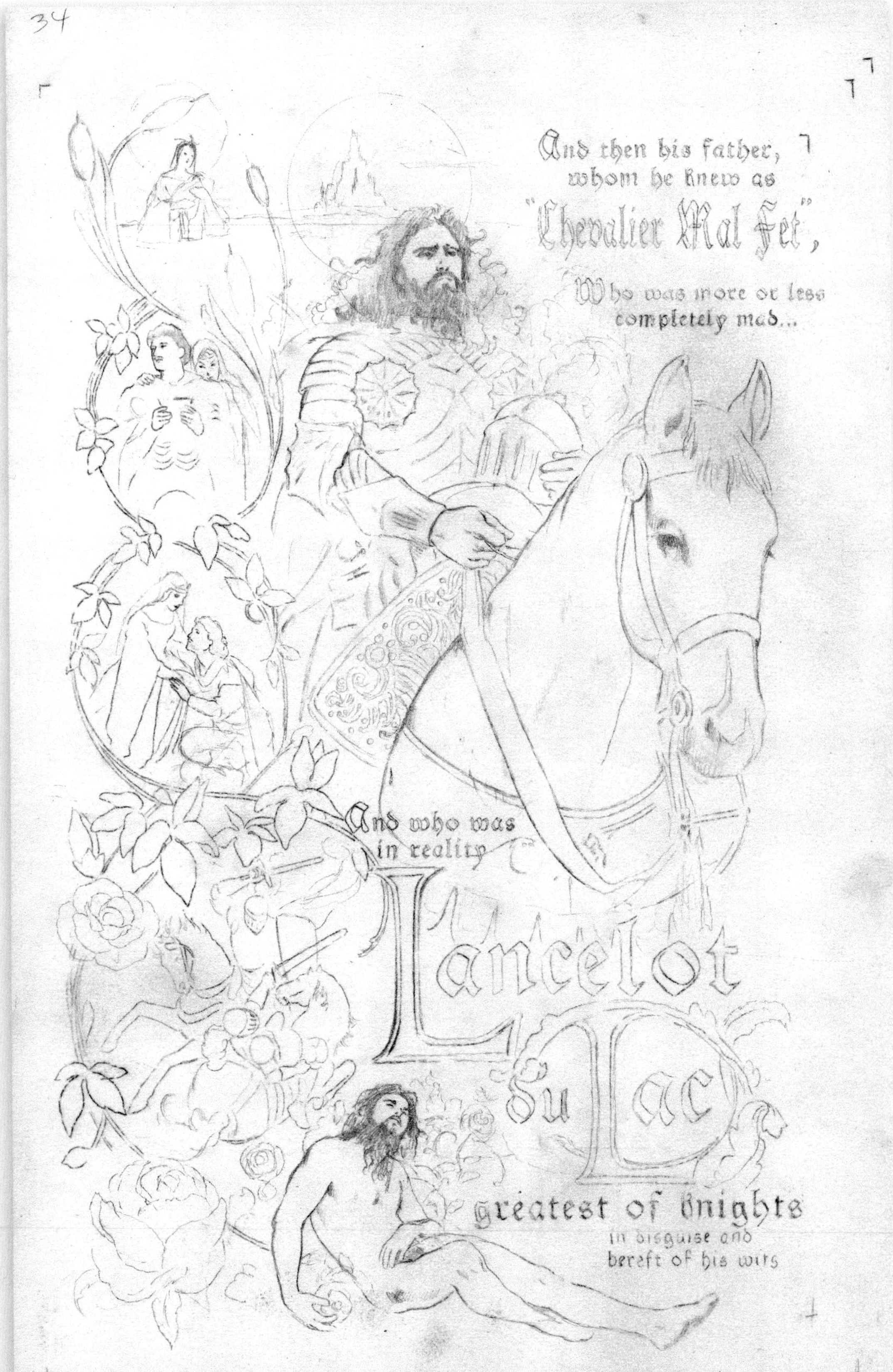
34
And then his father,
whom he knew as
"Chevalier Mal Fet",
Who was more or less
completely mad...
And who was
in reality
Lancelot
du Lac
greatest of knights
in disguise and
bereft of his wits

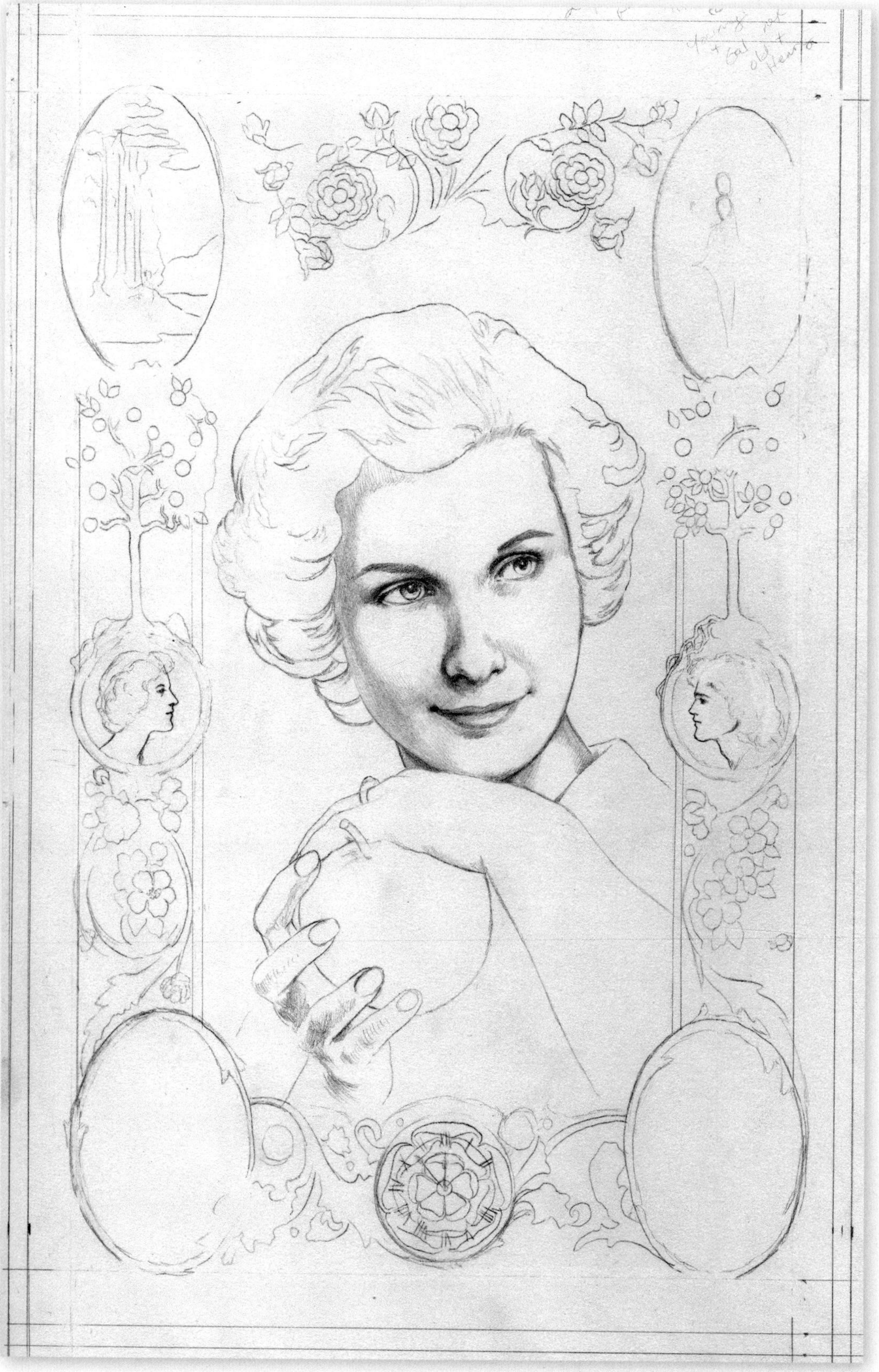

Galaad told Mrs. Whitaker

about his mother Elaine, who was flighty, and no better than she should have been, and something of a witch to boot.

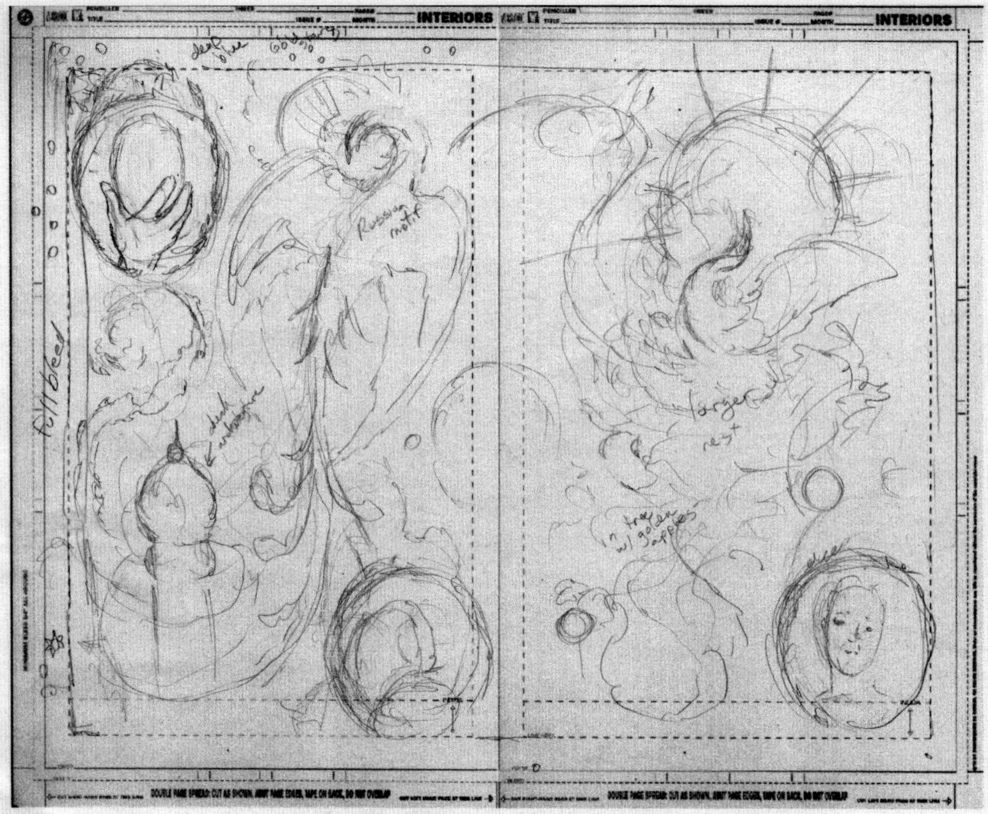
INTERIORS
INTERIORS
Russian motif
Full bleed
larger nest
in tree w/ golden apples
DOUBLE PAGE SPREAD: CUT AS SHOWN, ABUT PAGE EDGES, TAPE ON BACK, DO NOT OVERLAP
DOUBLE PAGE SPREAD: CUT AS SHOWN, ABUT PAGE EDGES, TAPE ON BACK, DO NOT OVERLAP

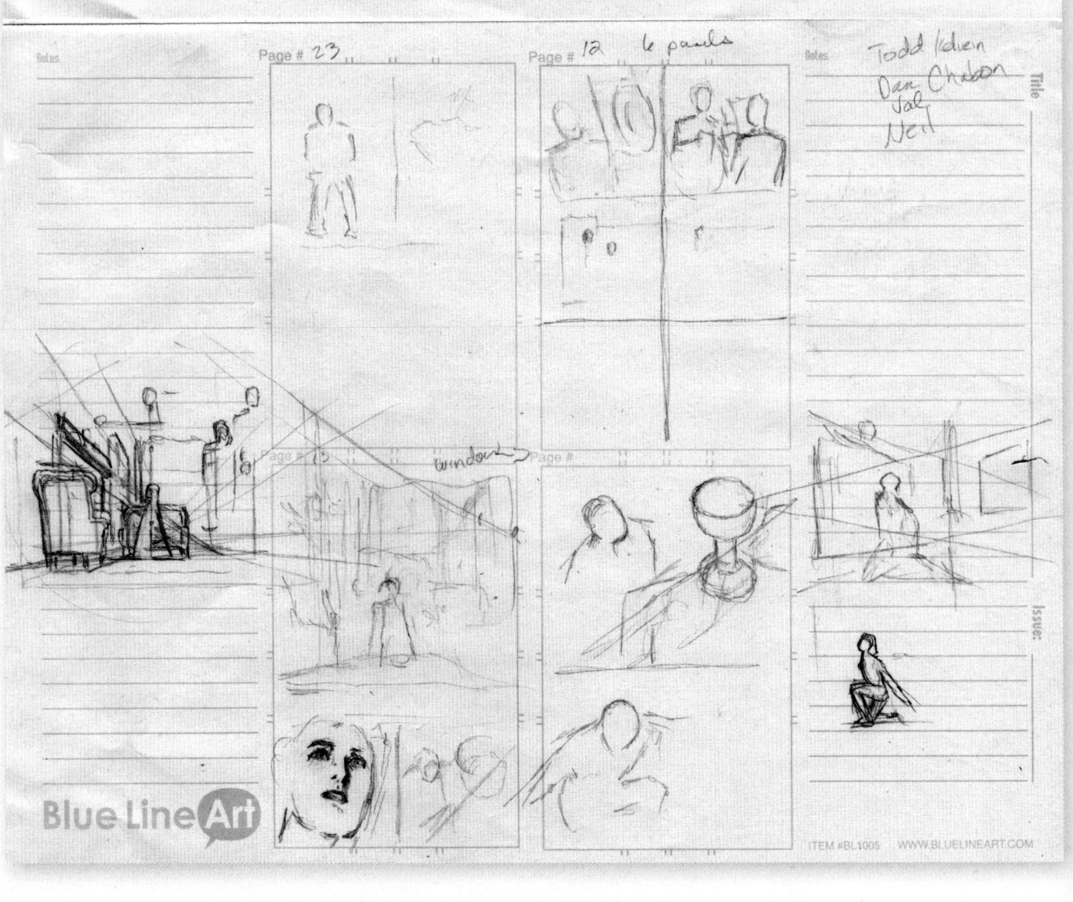
Notes
Page # 23
Page # 12
6 panels
Notes
Todd Klein
Val
Neil
Title
window
Page #
Page #
Issue:
Blue Line Art
ITEM #BL1005
WWW.BLUELINEART.COM

Notes:
Page #
Galaad
6-3"
5'4"
chair
mantle
couch
Notes:
Page #
Page #
Notes:
Blue Line Pro
ITEM #BL1005
WWW.BLUELINEPRO.C

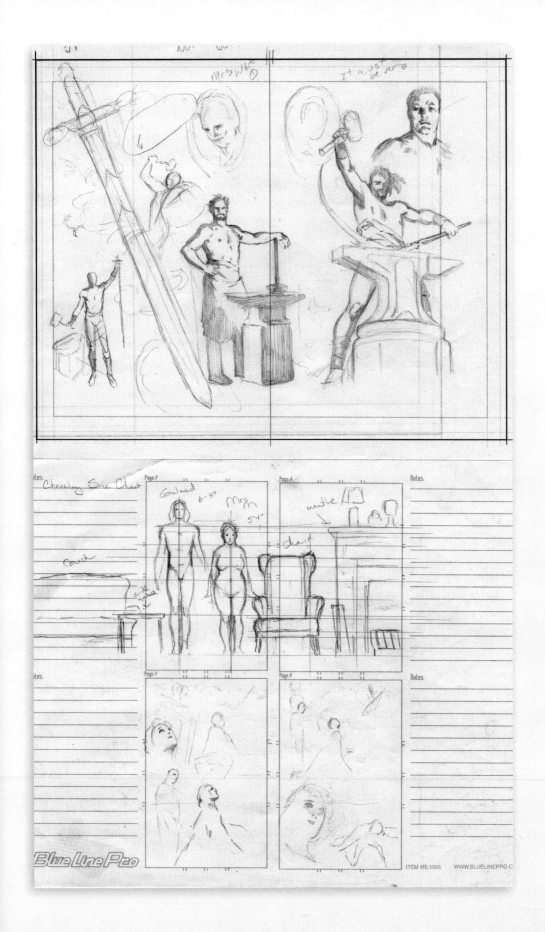

MORE TITLES FROM  THE NEIL GAIMAN LIBRARY

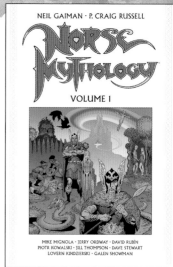

NEIL GAIMAN LIBRARY VOLUME 1
Collects *A Study in Emerald, Murder Mysteries, How to Talk to Girls at Parties,* and *Forbidden Bride*
Neil Gaiman and various artists
$49.99 | ISBN 978-1-50671-593-3

NEIL GAIMAN LIBRARY VOLUME 2
Collects *The Facts in the Departure of Miss Finch, Likely Stories, Harlequin Valentine,* and *Troll Bridge*
Neil Gaiman and various artists
$49.99 | ISBN 978-1-50671-594-0

NEIL GAIMAN LIBRARY VOLUME 3
Collects *Snow, Glass, Apples; The Problem of Susan; Only the End of the World Again;* and *Creatures of the Night*
Neil Gaiman and various artists
$49.99 | ISBN 978-1-50671-595-7

AMERICAN GODS: SHADOWS
Neil Gaiman, P. Craig Russell, Scott Hampton, and others
$29.99 | ISBN 978-1-50670-386-2

AMERICAN GODS: MY AINSEL
Neil Gaiman, P. Craig Russell, Scott Hampton, and others
$29.99 | ISBN 978-1-50670-730-3

**AMERICAN GODS:
THE MOMENT OF THE STORM**
Neil Gaiman, P. Craig Russell, Scott Hampton, and others
$29.99 | ISBN 978-1-50670-731-0

THE COMPLETE AMERICAN GODS
$124.99 | ISBN 978-1-50672-076-0

LIKELY STORIES
Neil Gaiman and Mark Buckingham
$17.99 | ISBN 978-1-50670-530-9

ONLY THE END OF THE WORLD AGAIN
Neil Gaiman, P. Craig Russell, and Troy Nixey
$19.99 | ISBN 978-1-50670-612-2

MURDER MYSTERIES
2nd Edition
Neil Gaiman, P. Craig Russell, and Lovern Kinderski
$19.99 | ISBN 978-1-61655-330-2

THE FACTS IN THE CASE OF THE DEPARTURE OF MISS FINCH
2nd Edition
Neil Gaiman and Michael Zulli
$13.99 | 978-1-61655-949-6

NEIL GAIMAN'S HOW TO TALK TO GIRLS AT PARTIES
Neil Gaiman, Fábio Moon, and Gabriel Bá
$17.99 | ISBN 978-1-61655-955-7

THE PROBLEM OF SUSAN AND OTHER STORIES
Neil Gaiman, P. Craig Russell, Paul Chadwick, and others
$17.99 | ISBN 978-1-50670-511-8

NEIL GAIMAN'S TROLL BRIDGE
Neil Gaiman and Colleen Doran
$14.99 | ISBN 978-1-50670-008-3

SIGNAL TO NOISE
Neil Gaiman and Dave McKean
$24.99 | ISBN 978-1-59307-752-5

CREATURES OF THE NIGHT
2nd Edition
Neil Gaiman and Michael Zulli
$12.99 | ISBN 978-1-50670-025-0

FORBIDDEN BRIDES OF THE FACELESS SLAVES IN THE SECRET HOUSE OF THE NIGHT OF DREAD DESIRE
Neil Gaiman and Shane Oakley
$17.99 | ISBN 978-1-50670-140-0

HARLEQUIN VALENTINE
2nd Edition
Neil Gaiman and John Bolton
$12.99 | ISBN 978-1-50670-087-8

NEIL GAIMAN'S A STUDY IN EMERALD
Neil Gaiman and Rafael Albuquerque
$17.99 | ISBN 978-1-50670-393-0

SNOW, GLASS, APPLES
Neil Gaiman and Colleen Doran
$17.99 | ISBN 978-1-50670-979-6

NORSE MYTHOLOGY VOLUME 1
Neil Gaiman, P. Craig Russell, Mike Mignola, and various artists
$29.99 | ISBN 978-1-50671-874-3

NORSE MYTHOLOGY VOLUME 2
$29.99 | ISBN 978-1-50672-217-7

AVAILABLE AT YOUR LOCAL COMICS SHOP OR BOOKSTORE.
To find a comics shop in your area, visit comicshoplocator.com. For more information, visit DarkHorse.com